Ninja Swirl
by CREAMi
Cookbook for Beginners

Master the Art of Frozen Delights with Simple & Delicious Ninja Swirl Recipes | Create Flavorful Soft Serve, Ice Cream, Sorbet, Milkshakes, and Gelato Anytime

Martha Justice

Table of Contents

Introduction

The Ninja Swirl by Creami and its accompanying cookbook offer an exciting and convenient way to enjoy delicious frozen desserts from the comfort of your home. Whether you're craving creamy ice cream, frosty sorbets, or rich milkshakes, this versatile kitchen tool allows you to create a wide variety of frozen treats in minutes. With its unique functionality, the Ninja Swirl by Creami makes it easier than ever to whip up healthy, flavorful, and customized desserts that cater to your taste buds and dietary needs.

The Ninja Swirl Cookbook takes this innovation a step further, providing an extensive collection of recipes that are designed for every taste preference. From dairy-free alternatives to indulgent, creamy classics, the recipes offer something for everyone. This cookbook simplifies the process, offering step-by-step instructions that guarantee perfect results every time. If you're ready to elevate your dessert game, the Ninja Swirl and its cookbook are your go-to tools for effortless, tasty creations.

Fundamentals of Ninja Swirl

The Ninja Swirl by Creami is a versatile appliance designed to create delicious frozen treats. Its key function is the ability to turn everyday ingredients into creamy, smooth desserts, such as ice cream, gelato, milkshakes, and sorbets. It uses specialized technology to transform frozen bases into frozen desserts by swirling the ingredients with precision.

What sets the Ninja Swirl apart is its simplicity and efficiency. It provides an easy-to-use approach for beginners and experts alike, delivering consistently creamy, restaurant-quality results in the comfort of your kitchen. With the Ninja Swirl, it's easier than ever to control the ingredients, flavors, and textures, making it a perfect choice for healthier and customizable frozen desserts.

What Is Ninja Swirl?

Ninja Swirl is a cutting-edge appliance that allows you to create frozen desserts at home in just minutes. Part of the Ninja Creami family, this machine is designed to blend and swirl frozen ingredients into smooth, creamy frozen treats like ice cream, soft serve, sorbet, gelato, and milkshakes. It operates by taking frozen ingredients, such as fruits, milk, or yogurt, and using advanced technology to churn them into desserts with perfect texture and consistency.

The device is extremely user-friendly, featuring easy-to-follow settings that ensure every batch is a success. With the Ninja Swirl, you can customize your treats by adding your favorite ingredients, whether you're looking for dairy-free, mix-ins, or low-fat options. This appliance also allows you to experiment with various flavors and textures, from chunky, ice cream-like consistency to velvety smooth gelato.

In addition, the Ninja Swirl is designed for convenience. It's quick to set up, simple to clean, and a perfect addition to any kitchen, whether you're serving up dessert for one or making a batch for the whole family. Whether you're an experienced chef or a beginner, the Ninja Swirl allows everyone to enjoy delicious, frozen creations with ease.

Functions

Scoop Programs

For those who prefer traditional, scoopable ice cream, the Scoop Program is a game-changer. This setting mimics the slow churn of artisanal ice cream makers, creating a dense, creamy texture that's perfect for cones, bowls, or sundaes. It's ideal for experimenting with mix-ins like cookie dough, nuts, or fruit swirls. Plus, the program's precise temperature control ensures your ice cream freezes evenly without icy crystals, delivering a professional-quality treat every time.

- **Ice Cream:** Designed for traditionally indulgent recipes. Great for turning dairy and dairy-alternative recipes into thick, creamy, scoopable ice creams.
- **Lite Ice Cream:** Designed for the health conscious to make keto, paleo, and vegan recipes that are low in sugar and/or fat or use sugar substitutes.
- **Sorbet:** Transform fruit-based recipes with high water and sugar content into creamy delights.

- **Gelato:** Transforms cooked bases into rich, dense, Italian style ice cream.
- **Frozen Yogurt:** Easily transform your favorite store-bought yogurts into healthy, creamy frozen treats with the touch of a button. When making frozen yogurt, ensure you are using full-fat yogurt with added sugar. Do not process nonfat yogurt or yogurt with no added sugar.
- **Milkshake:** Designed to create quick and thick milkshakes by combining your favorite ice cream (store bought or homemade), milk, and mix-ins.
- **Mix-In:** Designed to fold in pieces of candies, cookies, nuts, cereal, or frozen fruit to customize a just-processed base or store-bought treat.

Soft Serve Programs

The Soft Serve Program is perfect for creating smooth, velvety soft-serve ice cream right at home. Simply blend your favorite ingredients—like milk, cream, and flavorings—and let the Ninja Swirl work its magic. The machine churns the mixture at the ideal speed and temperature, delivering a light, airy texture that rivals your favorite ice cream shop. Whether you're craving classic vanilla, rich chocolate, or a fruity twist, this program ensures a flawless result every time.

- **Ice Cream:** Designed to bring the ice cream shop home. Expand upon classic soft-serve vanilla and chocolate for a whole new world of light, airy, fun flavors.
- **Lite Ice Cream:** Take classic soft-serve recipes to the next level with lower-fat, lower-sugar, and/or sugar-substitute options. Choose when processing paleo or vegan recipes.
- **Fruit Whip:** Fruit Whip has the consistency of soft-serve but uses a dairy-free fruit base, resulting in a sweet, tangy fruit flavor for a light, refreshing treat.
- **Frozen Custard:** Elevate custard-based recipes with richer, creamier, swirlable textures.

- **Frozen Yogurt:** Create yogurt-shop quality treats ready for dispensing. Mix your favorite store-bought yogurts with milk and spin to create light, airy, fro-yo-shaped results.

Scoop/Soft Serve Programs Creamifit: A unique program for high-protein, lower-calorie, low-sugar bases. Offers a faster, longer program to whip air through ingredients at the touch of a button.

Re-Spin: Designed to ensure a smooth texture after running one of the one-touch programs. Re-spin is often needed when the base is very cold (-7°F [-22°C]) and the texture is crumbly rather than creamy.

With the Ninja Swirl by Creami, you can explore endless flavor possibilities and enjoy healthier, customizable desserts anytime. Whether you're a soft-serve lover or a traditional ice cream enthusiast, this versatile machine has you covered!

Before First Use

Before you start creating delicious frozen treats with your Ninja Swirl, it's important to properly prepare your appliance. First, unbox the Ninja Swirl and make sure all the parts are accounted for. The main components typically include the motor base, the outer bowl, the bowl lid, and the paddle. It's also a good idea to check for any specific accessories like the storage container for your frozen dessert.

Start by thoroughly cleaning the machine. Wash the outer bowl, lid, and paddle with warm, soapy water, making sure to dry everything well after cleaning. You can also wipe down the motor base with a damp cloth to ensure there is no debris or residue left from the packaging process. Do not submerge the motor base in water as this could damage the electrical components.

Next, ensure that the motor base is set on a flat, stable surface. The Ninja Swirl operates best on a sturdy counter or table.

Double-check that the outer bowl is properly placed onto the motor base and that the paddle is securely in place before you begin any blending or mixing.

Before using the Ninja Swirl for the first time, it's helpful to familiarize yourself with the settings and functions. Review the user manual to understand how to use the different features, such as the blending speed and consistency options. This will ensure you achieve the perfect texture for your frozen treats.

Lastly, prepare your ingredients before starting. For best results, make sure that your ingredients are properly frozen and cut into small pieces to promote smoother blending. With everything ready, you're all set to enjoy the delicious world of frozen treats!

Step-By-Step Using It

Using the Ninja Swirl to create frozen treats is easy and fun. Follow these simple steps to make sure you're using your appliance correctly for smooth, creamy results every time:

Prepare Your Ingredients: Start by preparing your frozen base. Whether you're making ice cream, sorbet, or gelato, make sure your ingredients are properly frozen in chunks or cubes. This makes blending easier and faster. Some recipes may require a bit of pre-mixing or flavoring before freezing.

Set Up the Ninja Swirl: Place the motor base on a flat, stable surface in your kitchen. Ensure that it is clean and free from any debris. Attach the outer bowl and ensure it is securely locked into place.

Add Ingredients to the Swirl pint: Add your frozen ingredients into the Swirl pint and place the pint in the outer bowl. Be careful not to past the Max Fill line; leave some space for the ingredients to move around as they're blended. For best results, follow the recommended ingredient amounts in your recipe.

Select the Correct Setting: Depending on the type of frozen treat you are making, select the appropriate blending setting. The Ninja Swirl offers different speed settings for varying textures, such as a creamy gelato or chunkier sorbet.

Blend Your Frozen Treats: With the ingredients in place, press the button to start the blending process. The motor will start to swirl and blend the frozen items into a smooth consistency. Depending on your desired texture, this should take just a couple of minutes.

Check the Consistency: Once the blending is complete, check the texture. If you want a smoother consistency, you can run the machine for a few more seconds. If you prefer a chunkier consistency, stop when you've achieved the desired results.

Serve or Store: Once you're satisfied with the texture, scoop your delicious creation into bowls or cones and serve immediately. If you prefer, you can transfer the treat into an airtight container and store it in the freezer for later.

Clean-Up: Once you've finished making your frozen treat, remember to clean the Ninja Swirl. Wash the outer bowl, paddle, and lid with warm, soapy water, and wipe down the motor base. This will keep your appliance in good working condition for future use.

By following these simple steps, you can create a variety of delicious frozen desserts with ease and precision using your Ninja Swirl. Enjoy the endless flavor possibilities!

Benefits of Using the Ninja Swirl

The Ninja Swirl is a versatile and efficient appliance that brings the fun and creativity of frozen desserts right into your kitchen. Whether you're craving ice cream, sorbet, or frozen yogurt, the Ninja Swirl makes the process simple, fast, and enjoyable. Here are several benefits of using the Ninja Swirl:

1. Convenience and Speed

One of the most significant advantages of using the Ninja Swirl is its speed. Unlike traditional ice cream makers that require hours of freezing or churning, the Ninja Swirl can make smooth, creamy frozen treats in a matter of minutes. The high-powered motor and easy-to-use design help you create delicious desserts quickly, even if you're short on time. Simply add your ingredients, select the appropriate blending setting, and let the machine work its magic.

2. Healthier Homemade Options

Using the Ninja Swirl enables you to create healthier versions of your favorite frozen desserts. You have full control over the ingredients, so you can opt for natural sweeteners, fresh fruits, and lower-fat dairy options. This is ideal for those who are following specific diets like keto, vegan, or gluten-free. With the Ninja Swirl, you can customize your treats to fit your dietary needs without compromising on flavor. Say goodbye to the preservatives and artificial ingredients found in store-bought frozen desserts.

3. Customizable Textures and Flavors

The Ninja Swirl offers customizable settings that allow you to control the texture of your frozen treats. Whether you prefer smooth, creamy ice cream or chunkier, fruit-filled sorbet, the machine can blend the ingredients to your preferred consistency. Additionally, you can experiment with a wide variety of flavors, from traditional vanilla to more adventurous options like green veggies or salted caramel. The machine's versatility makes it easy to try out new recipes and tailor each treat to your tastes.

4. Easy to Use and Clean

The Ninja Swirl is designed with user-friendliness in mind. The straightforward controls make it simple to operate, even for beginners. You don't need any prior experience to create delicious frozen desserts. Additionally, cleaning the machine is a breeze. The removable components, including the bowl and paddle, can be easily washed with warm, soapy water. This makes maintenance quick and convenient, so you can focus more on enjoying your treats than on cleaning up afterward.

5. Cost-Effective

Buying store-bought frozen desserts can get expensive, especially if you're indulging in premium brands or specialty options. With the Ninja Swirl, you can save money in the long run by making your desserts at home. Ingredients like fresh fruit, yogurt, or milk are typically less expensive than packaged frozen treats. By using the Ninja Swirl, you can enjoy frozen desserts on a budget without sacrificing quality or taste.

6. Creative and Fun for All Ages

The Ninja Swirl is not only practical but also fun for the whole family. Children and adults alike will enjoy experimenting with different flavors, textures, and toppings. You can create personalized treats for parties, family gatherings, or as a fun weekend activity. It's a great way to bond with loved ones while indulging in delicious homemade desserts.

7. Compact and Space-Saving

Another benefit of the Ninja Swirl is its compact size. Unlike bulky ice cream machines, this appliance is small and easy to store, making it perfect for kitchens with limited counter space. Its sleek design ensures it doesn't take up much room in your kitchen, and it's portable enough to be taken out whenever you're ready to create frozen treats.

In conclusion, the Ninja Swirl offers numerous benefits that make it an excellent addition to any kitchen. Its speed, convenience, customizable settings, and health-conscious options make it a standout appliance for anyone who loves frozen desserts. Whether you're making a quick snack or hosting a party, the Ninja Swirl makes creating your favorite treats easy, fun, and enjoyable.

Parts and Accessories

The Ninja Swirl is designed with several essential parts and accessories that make creating frozen treats both easy and fun. Here's a quick overview:

Motor Base: The motor base is the heart of the Ninja Swirl. It powers the device, providing the necessary strength to blend frozen ingredients into smooth, creamy desserts.

Outer Bowl Lid: This lid is used to securely cover the outer bowl during the blending process, preventing any mess while ensuring that everything stays in place.

Creamerize Paddle: The creamerize paddle is designed to mix and transform frozen ingredients into a perfect creamy texture. It helps create smooth and thick frozen desserts.

Swirl Lid: This lid helps seal the ingredients inside the outer bowl, allowing the Ninja Swirl to work its magic by blending and swirls them into your favorite frozen treat.

Swirl Pint: The swirl pint is a convenient container used to store your homemade treats once they're ready, allowing for easy serving and storage.

Outer Bowl: The outer bowl is the main container where ingredients are placed for blending. It's designed for easy use and cleaning.

Dispense Lid: The dispense lid helps control the flow of the finished frozen treat like soft serve, making serving more convenient and mess-free.

These parts work together to ensure that making frozen desserts is seamless and enjoyable every time.

Tips and Tricks of Using the Ninja Swirl

The Ninja Swirl is a powerful and versatile appliance designed to create delicious frozen desserts, such as ice cream, sorbet, and frozen yogurt. Here are some tips and tricks to help you get the most out of your Ninja Swirl and ensure your frozen treats are always a hit.

Use Frozen Ingredients

For the best results, always use frozen fruits or ingredients when making your treats. The Ninja Swirl works best with frozen ingredients, as it helps achieve a smooth, creamy consistency in less time. Simply freeze your fruits or base ingredients overnight before blending.

Pre-Chill Your Ingredients

If you want to make sure your frozen treats have the perfect texture, chill your ingredients for at least an hour before placing them in the Ninja Swirl. This ensures that the ingredients blend better and the treat maintains its firmness.

Experiment with Flavors

The Ninja Swirl allows you to get creative with flavors. Don't be afraid to experiment with different fruits, extracts, and flavorings. Add vanilla, cinnamon, or cocoa powder to enhance your base. You can even mix in chocolate chips, nuts, or fresh berries after blending for added texture.

Use the Right Consistency

Sometimes, your frozen treat may come out too soft or too hard. If your creation is too soft, try adding a little more frozen fruit or ice and blend again. If it's too firm, let it sit for a few minutes before serving, or add a splash of liquid like milk or almond milk.

Make Frozen Yogurt and Shakes

While the Ninja Swirl is great for frozen desserts, you can also use it to make frozen yogurt and milkshakes. Blend frozen fruits with yogurt or milk to create a thick, creamy drink. You can even add protein powder or other supplements for a nutritious snack.

Keep It Clean

After using the Ninja Swirl, clean it promptly to ensure it stays in great condition. The bowl, paddle, and lids are all removable and can be washed easily with warm, soapy water. Avoid using harsh abrasives that could damage the surfaces.

Use Portion Control

When making treats like ice cream, it's easy to get carried away with portion sizes. Use the Ninja Swirl's measuring features or simply scoop a reasonable portion to avoid overindulging. By practicing portion control, you can enjoy your favorite desserts while keeping your calories in check.

Freeze Leftovers

If you make extra frozen treats, don't throw them out. Store the leftovers in the Swirl pint container, and keep them in the freezer for later. This is a great way to have ready-to-go homemade frozen treats whenever you want.

Perfect for Special Diets

The Ninja Swirl is perfect for those on special diets like keto, vegan, or gluten-free. Use non-dairy alternatives like almond or coconut milk, and sweeten with natural sweeteners like stevia or monk fruit. You can create personalized desserts that fit your dietary needs without compromising on taste.

By following these tips and tricks, you can maximize the potential of your Ninja Swirl, ensuring that every batch of frozen treats is a smooth, flavorful success.

Clean and Maintenance

Proper cleaning and maintenance are essential to ensuring that your Ninja Swirl remains in optimal working condition. Here's a step-by-step guide to cleaning and maintaining your Ninja Swirl after every use:

Turn Off and Unplug the Device

Always ensure that the Ninja Swirl is turned off and unplugged before starting the cleaning process. This is an important safety measure to avoid any accidents while cleaning.

Remove All Attachments

Carefully detach the outer bowl, creamerize paddle, and lid from the motor base. These parts are designed for easy removal and cleaning.

Wash the Removable Parts

Once detached, wash the removable parts (outer bowl, paddle, lid) with warm, soapy water. A soft sponge or cloth should be used to avoid scratching the surfaces. Avoid using abrasive scrubbers or harsh chemicals, as they can damage the parts. If any food residue is stuck, soak the parts in warm water for a few minutes to loosen them before cleaning.

Clean the Motor Base

To clean the motor base, use a damp cloth to wipe down the surface. Be sure not to let any water or moisture enter the motor. If necessary, use a dry microfiber cloth to remove any dust or residue. Never submerge the motor base in water or place it in the dishwasher.

Dry Everything Thoroughly

After washing all components, dry them thoroughly with a clean towel. Allow any parts that require air drying (like the paddle or outer bowl) to air dry completely before reassembling.

Store Properly

After cleaning and drying, store your Ninja Swirl in a cool, dry place. Avoid exposing it to excessive heat or moisture, as this could lead to damage over time.

Regular Maintenance

To maintain your Ninja Swirl's performance, it's important to periodically check for any build-up of residue or food particles. If necessary, use a gentle brush to clean small areas or hard-to-reach spots, especially around the paddle. Always ensure that no food particles remain, as they can affect the performance of the appliance.

Following these simple steps will help keep your Ninja Swirl in good working condition, allowing you to enjoy smooth, delicious frozen treats for years to come.

Frequently Asked Questions

1. How do I use the Ninja Swirl?

Using the Ninja Swirl is easy! Simply add your frozen ingredients into the swirl pint in the outer bowl, attach the creamerize paddle, and secure the lid. Turn the motor base on, and let the machine work its magic to transform your ingredients into creamy frozen treats. It's that simple!

2. Can I use fresh ingredients with the Ninja Swirl?

The Ninja Swirl is designed to work best with frozen ingredients. Fresh fruits and ingredients need to be frozen beforehand to achieve the desired creamy texture. It's recommended to freeze your ingredients for several hours before use.

3. How do I clean the Ninja Swirl?

After each use, unplug the machine, remove the outer bowl, paddle, and lid, and wash these removable parts with warm, soapy water. Use a damp cloth to clean the motor base. Allow everything to dry completely before reassembling.

4. Can I make dairy-free frozen treats with the Ninja Swirl?

Yes! The Ninja Swirl is perfect for making dairy-free frozen treats. You can use non-dairy alternatives like almond milk, coconut milk, or oat milk, along with your favorite frozen fruits to create a variety of dairy-free desserts.

5. Can I make ice cream with the Ninja Swirl?

Absolutely! The Ninja Swirl is designed to create creamy, ice cream-like textures from frozen ingredients, such as fruits, yogurt, or even dairy-free substitutes. You can easily make custom ice cream flavors and experiment with different textures.

6. How long does it take to make frozen treats with the Ninja Swirl?

The process is quick! Typically, it takes about 5 to 10 minutes to turn frozen ingredients into smooth, creamy frozen treats, depending on the type and amount of ingredients used.

7. Can I store leftover frozen treats?

Yes! If you have leftovers, simply transfer them into an airtight container and store them in the freezer. The Ninja Swirl's creations will remain frozen and ready for you to enjoy later.

Chapter 1 Soft Serve & Ice Creams

Orange Ice Cream

Prep Time: 10 minutes | Serves: 4

Ingredients:

1 cup heavy cream
½ cup orange juice
⅓ cup light brown sugar
2 tablespoons cream cheese frosting
1 teaspoon vanilla extract

Preparation:

1. In a bowl, put in heavy cream and remaining ingredients and whisk to incorporate thoroughly.
2. Pour the mixture into an empty Swirl Pint. Place storage lid on pint and freeze for at least 24 hours.
3. After 24 hours, remove the pint from the freezer and take off the lid. Place the Swirl Pint in the outer bowl, then lock the outer bowl lid into place.
4. Transfer the outer bowl into the machine, twisting it into place.
5. Press the power button to turn on the unit. Select Scoop. Then select Ice Cream. Let the cycle complete.
6. Lift the Swirl Pint out of the outer bowl.
7. Transfer the ice cream into serving bowls and enjoy immediately.

Per Serving: Calories: 191 | Fat: 12.4g | Sat Fat: 7.3g | Carbohydrates: 19.8g | Fiber: 0.1g | Sugar: 17.7g | Protein: 0.8g

Blueberry Soft Serve

Prep Time: 10 minutes | Serves: 4

Ingredients:

1 cup whole milk
1¼ cups frozen blueberries
1 teaspoon vanilla extract

Preparation:

1. In a high-powered blender, put in milk and remaining ingredients and process to form a smooth mixture.
2. Pour the mixture into an empty Swirl Pint. Place storage lid on pint and freeze for at least 24 hours.
3. After 24 hours, remove the pint from the freezer and take off the lid. Place the Swirl Pint in the outer bowl, then lock the outer bowl lid into place.
4. Transfer the outer bowl into the machine, twisting it into place.
5. Press the power button to turn on the unit. Select Soft Serve. Then select Ice Cream. Let the cycle complete.
6. Remove the pint from the outer bowl, then attach the soft serve dispensing lid to the pint.
7. Match the blue line on the dispensing lid with the blue line on the dispensing side of the machine, then insert the pint into the machine and twist to lock it into place.
8. Twist the white base of the pint until it is in the "Open" position.
9. Dispense and serve.

Per Serving: Calories: 66 | Fat: 2.1g | Sat Fat: 1.1g | Carbohydrates: 9.5g | Fiber: 1.1g | Sugar: 7.8g | Protein: 2.3g

Green Tea Soft Serve

Ingredients:

1 cup cashew milk
3 green tea bags
1 cup coconut milk
½ cup sugar
2 tablespoons cream cheese
¼ teaspoon salt

Preparation:

1. In a medium-sized saucepan, put in cashew milk on burner at around medium heat and cook until simmering.
2. Take off saucepan from burner and add in tea bags.
3. Cover the pan and let it steep until cooled thoroughly.
4. After cooling, squeeze the tea bags into the milk.
5. Then discard the tea bags.
6. In a high-powered blender, put in green tea milk, coconut milk, sugar, cream cheese and salt and remaining ingredients and process to form a smooth mixture.
7. Pour the mixture into an empty Swirl Pint. Place storage lid on pint and freeze for at least 24 hours.
8. After 24 hours, remove the pint from the freezer and take off the lid. Place the Swirl Pint in the outer bowl, then lock the outer bowl lid into place.
9. Transfer the outer bowl into the machine, twisting it into place.
10. Press the power button to turn on the unit. Select Soft Serve. Then select Ice Cream. Let the cycle complete.
11. Remove the pint from the outer bowl, then attach the soft serve dispensing lid to the pint.
12. Match the blue line on the dispensing lid with the blue line on the dispensing side of the machine, then insert the pint into the machine and twist to lock it into place.
13. Twist the white base of the pint until it is in the "Open" position.
14. Dispense and serve.

Per Serving: Calories: 255 | Fat: 16.5g | Sat Fat: 13.8g | Carbohydrates: 28.7g | Fiber: 1.3g | Sugar: 27g | Protein: 1.8g

Strawberry Ice Cream

Ingredients:

1 cup heavy cream
1½ cups fresh strawberries, sliced
3 tablespoons sugar
1 teaspoon vanilla extract

Preparation:

1. In a bowl, put in the heavy cream and whisk until smooth.
2. Put in strawberry slices and with the back of a fork, lightly mash them.
3. Add in the sugar and vanilla extract and blend to incorporate thoroughly.
4. Pour mixture into an empty Swirl Pint. Place storage lid on pint and freeze for at least 24 hours.
5. After 24 hours, remove the pint from the freezer and take off the lid. Place the Swirl Pint in the outer bowl, then lock the outer bowl lid into place.
6. Transfer the outer bowl into the machine, twisting it into place.
7. Press the power button to turn on the unit. Select Scoop. Then select Ice Cream. Let the cycle complete.
8. Lift the Swirl Pint out of the outer bowl.
9. Transfer the ice cream into serving bowls and enjoy immediately.

Per Serving: Calories: 158 | Fat: 11.3g | Sat Fat: 6.9g | Carbohydrates: 14.1g | Fiber: 1.1g | Sugar: 11.8g | Protein: 1g

Peanut Butter Vanilla Soft Serve

Ingredients:

1¾ cups milk, skimmed
¼ cup stevia-cane sugar blend
3 tablespoons smooth peanut butter
1 teaspoon vanilla extract

Preparation:

1. In a bowl, merge together all the ingredients and thoroughly whisk.
2. Pour mixture into an empty Swirl Pint. Snap the lid on the pint and freeze for at least 24 hours.
3. After 24 hours, remove the pint from the freezer and take off the lid. Place the Swirl Pint in the outer bowl, then lock the outer bowl lid into place.
4. Transfer the outer bowl into the machine, twisting it into place.
5. Press the power button to turn on the unit. Select Soft Serve. Then select Ice Cream. Let the cycle complete.
6. Remove the pint from the outer bowl, then attach the soft serve dispensing lid to the pint,
7. Match the blue line on the dispensing lid with the blue line on the dispensing side of the machine, then insert the pint into the machine and twist to lock it into place.
8. Twist the white base of the pint until it is in the "Open" position.
9. Dispense and serve.

Per Serving: Calories: 143 | Fat: 6.1g | Sat Fat: 1.2g | Carbohydrates: 19.7g | Fiber: 0.7g | Sugar: 18.5g | Protein: 6.5g

Honey Pumpkin Soft Serve

Prep Time: 10 minutes | Serves: 4

Ingredients:

1¼ cups whole milk
1 teaspoon vanilla extract
½ cup pumpkin puree
1½ teaspoons pumpkin pie spice
¼ cup honey

Preparation:

1. In a bowl, put in milk and remaining ingredients and whisk until blended thoroughly.
2. Pour mixture into an empty Swirl Pint. Place storage lid on pint and freeze for at least 24 hours.
3. After 24 hours, remove the pint from the freezer and take off the lid. Place the Swirl Pint in the outer bowl, then lock the outer bowl lid into place.
4. Transfer the outer bowl into the machine, twisting it into place.
5. Press the power button to turn on the unit. Select Soft Serve. Then select Ice Cream. Let the cycle complete.
6. Remove the pint from the outer bowl, then attach the soft serve dispensing lid to the pint.
7. Match the blue line on the dispensing lid with the blue line on the dispensing side of the machine, then insert the pint into the machine and twist to lock it into place.
8. Twist the white base of the pint until it is in the "Open" position.
9. Dispense and serve.

Per Serving: Calories: 181 | Fat: 5.6g | Sat Fat: 3.2g | Carbohydrates: 28.1g | Fiber: 1g | Sugar: 27.4g | Protein: 5.8g

Sweet Potato Ice Cream

Prep Time: 15 minutes | Cook Time: 10 seconds | Serves: 4

Ingredients:

1 tablespoon cream cheese
5 tablespoons white sugar
½ tablespoon corn syrup
1 teaspoon ground cinnamon
1 teaspoon vanilla extract
1 cup whole milk
¾ cup heavy cream
3 tablespoons sweet potato puree

Preparation:

1. In a large-sized microwave-safe bowl, put in the cream cheese and microwave on High for about 10 seconds.
2. Take off from the microwave and blend until smooth.
3. Put in sugar, corn syrup, cinnamon and vanilla extract and with a wire whisk, beat until the mixture looks like frosting.
4. Slowly put in milk, heavy cream and sweet potato puree and whisk until blended thoroughly.
5. Pour the mixture into an empty Swirl Pint. Place storage lid on pint and freeze for at least 24 hours.
6. After 24 hours, remove the pint from the freezer and take off the lid. Place the Swirl Pint in the outer bowl, then lock the outer bowl lid into place.
7. Transfer the outer bowl into the machine, twisting it into place.
8. Press the power button to turn on the unit. Select Scoop. Then select Ice Cream. Let the cycle complete.
9. Lift the Swirl Pint out of the outer bowl.
10. Transfer the ice cream into serving bowls and enjoy immediately.
Per Serving: Calories: 202 | Fat: 11.2g | Sat Fat: 6.9g | Carbohydrates: 23.6g | Fiber: 0.5g | Sugar: 19.7g | Protein: 2.9g

Pear Soft Serve

Prep Time: 15 minutes | Cook Time: 15 minutes | Serves: 4

Ingredients:

1 (14-ounce) can full-fat unsweetened coconut milk
3 medium pears, peeled, cored and cut into 1-inch pieces
½ cup sugar, granulated

Preparation:

1. In a saucepan, merge together all the ingredients and stir well.
2. Thoroughly boil and switch the heat to low, so that it simmers for 10 minutes.
3. Eliminate from the heat and blitz the mixture after it is cooled down.
4. Pour the mixture into an empty Swirl Pint. Snap the lid on the pint and freeze for at least 24 hours.
5. After 24 hours, remove the pint from the freezer and take off the lid. Place the Swirl Pint in the outer bowl, then lock the outer bowl lid into place.
6. Transfer the outer bowl into the machine, twisting it into place.
7. Press the power button to turn on the unit. Select Soft Serve. Then select Ice Cream. Let the cycle complete.
8. Remove the pint from the outer bowl, then attach the soft serve dispensing lid to the pint.
9. Match the blue line on the dispensing lid with the blue line on the dispensing side of the machine, then insert the pint into the machine and twist to lock it into place.
10. Twist the white base of the pint until it is in the "Open" position.
11. Dispense and serve.
Per Serving: Calories: 368 | Fat: 18.5g | Sat Fat: 168g | Carbohydrates: 51.9g | Fiber: 4.9g | Sugar: 41.8g | Protein: 2.1g

Lavender Ice Cream

Prep Time: 15 minutes | Cook Time: 25 minutes | Serves: 4

> **Ingredients:**

1 cup whole milk
1 cup heavy cream
2 tablespoons dried lavender
2 tablespoons honey
⅓ cup monk fruit sweetener
⅛ teaspoon salt

> **Preparation:**

1. In a medium saucepan, put in milk and heavy cream on burner at around medium heat and cook until heated through.
2. Put in lavender and cook for around 20 minutes.
3. Take off saucepan from burner and through a fine-mesh strainer, strain the mixture into a medium-sized bowl.
4. Put in honey, monk fruit sweetener and salt to bowl and whisk to incorporate thoroughly.
5. Pour the mixture into an empty Swirl Pint and place into an ice bath to cool. After cooling, place storage lid on pint and freeze for at least 24 hours.
6. After 24 hours, remove the pint from the freezer and take off the lid. Place the Swirl Pint in the outer bowl, then lock the outer bowl lid into place.
7. Transfer the outer bowl into the machine, twisting it into place.
8. Press the power button to turn on the unit. Select Scoop. Then select Ice Cream. Let the cycle complete.
9. Lift the Swirl Pint out of the outer bowl.
10. Transfer the ice cream into serving bowls and enjoy immediately.

Per Serving: Calories: 140 | Fat: 13.1g | Sat Fat: 8.1g | Carbohydrates: 3.6g | Fiber: 0g | Sugar: 3.2g | Protein: 2.6g

Lemon Coconut Ice Cream

Prep Time: 10 minutes | Serves: 4

> **Ingredients:**

¾ cup coconut milk
½ cup coconut cream
¼ cup frozen lemon juice concentrate
3½ tablespoons instant butterscotch pudding mix
2 tablespoons sugar
1 teaspoon vanilla extract

> **Preparation:**

1. In a large-sized bowl, put in coconut milk and remaining ingredients and whisk until blended thoroughly.
2. Pour the mixture into an empty Swirl Pint. Place storage lid on pint and freeze for at least 24 hours.
3. After 24 hours, remove the pint from the freezer and take off the lid. Place the Swirl Pint in the outer bowl, then lock the outer bowl lid into place.
4. Transfer the outer bowl into the machine, twisting it into place.
5. Press the power button to turn on the unit. Select Scoop. Then select Ice Cream. Let the cycle complete.
6. Lift the Swirl Pint out of the outer bowl.
7. Transfer the ice cream into serving bowls and enjoy immediately.

Per Serving: Calories: 353 | Fat: 30.8g | Sat Fat: 25.8g | Carbohydrates: 19.2g | Fiber: 1.4g | Sugar: 8.9g | Protein: 3.2g

Cinnamon Chocolate Soft Serve

Prep Time: 10 minutes | Serves: 4

Ingredients:

1 cup cottage cheese
1 cup chocolate milk
2 tablespoons honey
1 scoop chocolate protein powder
½ teaspoon vanilla extract
1 teaspoon ground cinnamon
Pinch of salt

Preparation:

1. In a high-powered blender, put in cottage cheese and remaining ingredients and process to form a smooth mixture.
2. Transfer the blended mixture into an empty Swirl Pint container.
3. Place storage lid on pint and freeze for at least 24 hours.
4. After 24 hours, remove the pint from the freezer and take off the lid. Place the Swirl Pint in the outer bowl, then lock the outer bowl lid into place.
5. Transfer the outer bowl into the machine, twisting it into place.
6. Press the power button to turn on the unit. Select Soft Serve. Then select Ice Cream.
7. Let the cycle complete. If it's not completely creamy after the first cycle, you can do a Re-spin cycle.
8. Remove the pint from the outer bowl, then attach the soft serve dispensing lid to the pint.
9. Match the blue line on the dispensing lid with the blue line on the dispensing side of the machine, then insert the pint into the machine and twist to lock it into place.
10. Twist the white base of the pint until it is in the "Open" position.
11. Dispense and serve.

Per Serving: Calories: 167 | Fat: 3.6g | Sat Fat: 2.3g | Carbohydrates: 18.8g | Fiber: 1g | Sugar: 15.4g | Protein: 15.2g

Banana Pudding Ice Cream

Prep Time: 10 minutes | Serves: 4

Ingredients:

1 cup cottage cheese
½ cup milk
4 tablespoons instant banana pudding mix
2 tablespoons heavy cream
1 tablespoon maple syrup
½ teaspoon banana extract

Preparation:

1. Place cottage cheese and remaining ingredients into a large-sized bowl and with an immersion blender, blend to incorporate.
2. Pour mixture into an empty Swirl Pint. Place storage lid on pint and freeze for at least 24 hours.
3. After 24 hours, remove the pint from the freezer and take off the lid. Place the Swirl Pint in the outer bowl, then lock the outer bowl lid into place.
4. Transfer the outer bowl into the machine, twisting it into place.
5. Press the power button to turn on the unit. Select Scoop. Then select Ice Cream. Let the cycle complete.
6. Lift the Swirl Pint out of the outer bowl and enjoy.

Per Serving: Calories: 212 | Fat: 6.2g | Sat Fat: 3.8g | Carbohydrates: 26.9g | Fiber: 0g | Sugar: 4.6g | Protein: 11.7g

Coconut Soft Serve

Prep Time: 15 minutes | Serves: 4

Ingredients:

1 (14-ounce) can full-fat coconut milk
½ cup granulated sugar
1 teaspoon vanilla extract

Preparation:

1. In a medium-sized bowl, put in coconut milk, sugar and vanilla extract and whisk to form smooth milk.
2. Pour the mixture into an empty Swirl Pint. Place storage lid on pint and freeze for at least 24 hours.
3. After 24 hours, remove the pint from the freezer and take off the lid. Place the Swirl Pint in the outer bowl, then lock the outer bowl lid into place.
4. Transfer the outer bowl into the machine, twisting it into place.
5. Press the power button to turn on the unit. Select Soft Serve. Then select Ice Cream. Let the cycle complete.
6. Remove the pint from the outer bowl, then attach the soft serve dispensing lid to the pint.
7. Match the blue line on the dispensing lid with the blue line on the dispensing side of the machine, then insert the pint into the machine and twist to lock it into place.
8. Twist the white base of the pint until it is in the "Open" position.
9. Dispense and serve.

Per Serving: Calories: 280 | Fat: 18.3g | Sat Fat: 16.8g | Carbohydrates: 28.2g | Fiber: 0g | Sugar: 26.7g | Protein: 1.5g

Strawberry Soft Serve

Prep Time: 10 minutes | Serves: 4

Ingredients:

1 (13¼-ounce) can full-fat coconut milk
⅓ cup strawberry jam
1 teaspoon vanilla extract

Preparation:

1. Place coconut milk and remaining ingredients in a medium bowl and whisk to incorporate thoroughly.
2. Pour mixture into an empty Swirl Pint. Place storage lid on pint and freeze for at least 24 hours.
3. After 24 hours, remove the pint from the freezer and take off the lid. Place the Swirl Pint in the outer bowl, then lock the outer bowl lid into place.
4. Transfer the outer bowl into the machine, twisting it into place.
5. Press the power button to turn on the unit. Select Soft Serve. Then select Ice Cream. Let the cycle complete.
6. Remove the pint from the outer bowl, then attach the soft serve dispensing lid to the pint.
7. Match the blue line on the dispensing lid with the blue line on the dispensing side of the machine, then insert the pint into the machine and twist to lock it into place.
8. Twist the white base of the pint until it is in the "Open" position.
9. Dispense and serve.

Per Serving: Calories: 281 | Fat: 17.7g | Sat Fat: 16.2g | Carbohydrates: 27.9g | Fiber: 0g | Sugar: 21.6g | Protein: 1.5g

Banana Ice Cream

Prep Time: 10 minutes | Serves: 4

Ingredients:

2 large ripe bananas, peeled and cut into small chunks
½ cup whole milk
½ cup heavy cream
3-4 drops liquid stevia
¾ teaspoon vanilla extract

Preparation:

1. In a large-sized high-powered blender, put in bananas and remaining ingredients and process to form a smooth mixture.
2. Pour mixture into an empty Swirl Pint. Place storage lid on pint and freeze for at least 24 hours.
3. After 24 hours, remove the pint from the freezer and take off the lid. Place the Swirl Pint in the outer bowl, then lock the outer bowl lid into place.
4. Transfer the outer bowl into the machine, twisting it into place.
5. Press the power button to turn on the unit. Select Scoop. Then select Ice Cream. Let the cycle complete.
6. Lift the Swirl Pint out of the outer bowl and enjoy.

Per Serving: Calories: 125 | Fat: 6.7g | Sat Fat: 4.1g | Carbohydrates: 15.4g | Fiber: 1.5g | Sugar: 8.9g | Protein: 1.9g

Lemon Ice Cream

Prep Time: 10 minutes | Serves: 4

Ingredients:

¼ cup lemon curd
2 tablespoons granulated sugar
2 tablespoons limoncello
1 cup heavy cream
¾ cup whole milk
1 teaspoon lemon zest, grated

Preparation:

1. In a large-sized bowl, put in lemon curd, sugar and limoncello and whisk to incorporate thoroughly.
2. Put in heavy cream, milk, and lemon zest and whisk to incorporate thoroughly.
3. Pour the mixture into an empty Swirl Pint. Place storage lid on pint and freeze for at least 24 hours.
4. After 24 hours, remove the pint from the freezer and take off the lid. Place the Swirl Pint in the outer bowl, then lock the outer bowl lid into place.
5. Transfer the outer bowl into the machine, twisting it into place.
6. Press the power button to turn on the unit. Select Scoop. Then select Ice Cream. Let the cycle complete.
7. Lift the Swirl Pint out of the outer bowl.
8. Transfer the ice cream into serving bowls and enjoy immediately.

Per Serving: Calories: 344 | Fat: 18.6g | Sat Fat: 10.8g | Carbohydrates: 13g | Fiber: 0g | Sugar: 12.5g | Protein: 3.1g

Peppermint Candy and Coconut Ice Cream

Prep Time: 10 minutes | Cook Time: 10 minutes | Serves: 4

Ingredients:

¾ cup peppermint candies, crushed
1 cup unsweetened coconut milk
1 (5.4-ounce) can coconut cream

Preparation:

1. Place peppermint candies and remaining ingredients in a small-sized saucepan over medium-high heat and whisk to incorporate thoroughly.
2. Cook for around 10 minutes.
3. Pour the mixture into an empty Swirl Pint and place into an ice bath to cool. After cooling, Place storage lid on pint and freeze for at least 24 hours.
4. After 24 hours, remove the pint from the freezer and take off the lid. Place the Swirl Pint in the outer bowl, then lock the outer bowl lid into place.
5. Transfer the outer bowl into the machine, twisting it into place.
6. Press the power button to turn on the unit. Select Scoop. Then select Ice Cream. Let the cycle complete.
7. Lift the Swirl Pint out of the outer bowl.
8. Transfer the ice cream into serving bowls and enjoy immediately.

Per Serving: Calories: 337 | Fat: 23.6g | Sat Fat: 20.8g | Carbohydrates: 33.1g | Fiber: 2.2g | Sugar: 21.1g | Protein: 2.3g

Taro Ice Cream

Prep Time: 15 minutes | Cook Time: 30 minutes | Serves: 5

Ingredients:

1 cup condensed milk, sweetened
½ lb. taro, peeled
1 cup heavy cream, chilled

Preparation:

1. Boil the taros for 30 minutes until tender, then drain them.
2. Move the boiled taros into an empty Swirl Pint along with heavy cream and condensed milk.
3. Snap the lid on the pint and freeze for at least 24 hours.
4. After 24 hours, remove the pint from the freezer and take off the lid. Place the Swirl Pint in the outer bowl, then lock the outer bowl lid into place.
5. Transfer the outer bowl into the machine, twisting it into place.
6. Press the power button to turn on the unit. Select Scoop. Then select Ice Cream. Let the cycle complete.
7. Lift the Swirl Pint out of the outer bowl.
8. Transfer the ice cream into serving bowls and enjoy immediately.

Per Serving: Calories: 330 | Fat: 14.3g | Sat Fat: 8.9g | Carbohydrates: 46g | Fiber: 1.9g | Sugar: 33.5g | Protein: 6g

Oreo Ice Cream

Prep Time: 15 minutes | Cook Time: 10 minutes | Serves: 4

Ingredients:

10 Oreos, roughly chopped
1 cup heavy cream
½ cup sugar
½ cup whole milk
1 teaspoon vanilla extract
3 egg yolks
⅛ teaspoon salt

Preparation:

1. In a saucepan, merge half the sugar with ½ cup of milk and salt.
2. Cook over medium heat until it starts simmering, then eliminate from heat.
3. In a small bowl, merge the egg yolks with sugar and remaining milk.
4. Move this mixture into the saucepan and cook for 5 minutes.
5. Eliminate the pot from heat and set aside to cool it down.
6. Merge in the cream, chopped cookies, and vanilla.
7. Pour the mixture into an empty Swirl Pint. Snap the lid on the pint and freeze for at least 24 hours.
8. After 24 hours, remove the pint from the freezer and take off the lid. Place the Swirl Pint in the outer bowl, then lock the outer bowl lid into place.
9. Transfer the outer bowl into the machine, twisting it into place.
10. Press the power button to turn on the unit. Scoop. Then select Ice Cream. Let the cycle complete.
11. Lift the Swirl Pint out of the outer bowl and enjoy.

Per Serving: Calories: 2109 | Fat: 105.5g | Sat Fat: 66.2g | Carbohydrates: 257.8g | Fiber: 2.5g | Sugar: 204.3g | Protein: 43.6g

Blackberry Soft Serve

Prep Time: 10 minutes | Cook Time: 5 minutes | Serves: 4

Ingredients:

1 cup fresh blackberries
¼ cup granulated sugar
1 cup whole milk
½ cup heavy whipping cream

Preparation:

1. In a small-sized saucepan, put in blackberries and sugar and blend to incorporate.
2. Place the pan of blackberries on burner at around medium heat and cook for approximately 3-5 minutes, stirring occasionally.
3. Take off the pan of blackberries from burner and transfer in to a small-sized bowl.
4. Set aside to cool for a few minutes.
5. In the bowl of blackberries, put in milk and heavy whipping cream and with an immersion blender, blend until smooth.
6. Pour mixture into an empty Swirl Pint. Place storage lid on pint and freeze for at least 24 hours.
7. After 24 hours, remove the pint from the freezer and take off the lid. Place the Swirl Pint in the outer bowl, then lock the outer bowl lid into place.
8. Transfer the outer bowl into the machine, twisting it into place.
9. Press the power button to turn on the unit. Select Soft Serve. Then select Ice Cream. Let the cycle complete.
10. Remove the pint from the outer bowl, then attach the soft serve dispensing lid to the pint.
11. Match the blue line on the dispensing lid with the blue line on the dispensing side of the machine, then insert the pint into the machine and twist to lock it into place.
12. Twist the white base of the pint until it is in the "Open" position.
13. Dispense and serve.

Per Serving: Calories: 151 | Fat: 7.7g | Sat Fat: 4.6g | Carbohydrates: 19.1g | Fiber: 1.9g | Sugar: 17.5g | Protein: 2.8g

Coffee Ice Cream

Prep Time: 15 minutes | Cook Time: 5 minutes | Serves: 4

Ingredients:

1 cup whole milk
2 tablespoons finely ground coffee
1 cup cream
1 tablespoon coffee liqueur
2 tablespoons agave nectar
⅓ cup monk fruit sweetener
1 teaspoon vanilla extract

Preparation:

1. In a medium-sized saucepan, put in milk on burner at around medium heat and cook until boiling.
2. Take off the saucepan of milk from burner and blend in coffee.
3. Let it steep for around 1 minute.
4. Put in cream, coffee liqueur, agave nectar, monk fruit sweetener and vanilla extract and whisk to incorporate thoroughly.
5. Pour the mixture into an empty Swirl Pint and place into an ice bath to cool. After cooling, place storage lid on pint and freeze for at least 24 hours.
6. After 24 hours, remove the pint from the freezer and take off the lid. Place the Swirl Pint in the outer bowl, then lock the outer bowl lid into place.
7. Transfer the outer bowl into the machine, twisting it into place.
8. Press the power button to turn on the unit. Select Scoop. Then select Ice Cream. Let the cycle complete.
9. Lift the Swirl Pint out of the outer bowl.
10. Transfer the ice cream into serving bowls and enjoy immediately.
Per Serving: Calories: 122 | Fat: 5.3g | Sat Fat: 3.2g | Carbohydrates: 14.8g | Fiber: 0.5g | Sugar: 14.1g | Protein: 2.5g

Vanilla Ice Cream

Prep Time: 10 minutes | Serves: 4

Ingredients:

1 cup milk
½ cup heavy cream
⅓ cup sugar
1 teaspoon vanilla extract

Preparation:

1. In a high-powered blender, put in milk and remaining ingredients and process to form a smooth mixture.
2. Pour the mixture into an empty Swirl Pint. Place storage lid on pint and freeze for at least 24 hours.
3. After 24 hours, remove the pint from the freezer and take off the lid. Place the Swirl Pint in the outer bowl, then lock the outer bowl lid into place.
4. Transfer the outer bowl into the machine, twisting it into place.
5. Press the power button to turn on the unit. Select Scoop. Then select Ice Cream. Let the cycle complete.
6. Lift the Swirl Pint out of the outer bowl.
7. Transfer the ice cream into serving bowls and enjoy immediately.
Per Serving: Calories: 148 | Fat: 6.8g | Sat Fat: 4.2g | Carbohydrates: 20.2g | Fiber: 0g | Sugar: 19.6g | Protein: 2.3g

Carrot Ice Cream

Ingredients:

2 cups heavy cream
½ cup sugar, granulated
¾ teaspoon kosher salt
2 teaspoons apple cider vinegar
2 cups whole milk
⅓ cup light brown sugar
4 carrots, peeled and chopped

Preparation:

1. In a saucepan, merge together the cream, milk, sugars, and salt.
2. Whisk over low heat and stir in the carrots.
3. Cook the carrots until they are tender.
4. Move the mixture into an empty Swirl Pint after letting it cool down. Merge in the vinegar and salt.
5. Place storage lid on pint and freeze for at least 24 hours.
6. After 24 hours, remove the pint from the freezer and take off the lid. Place the Swirl Pint in the outer bowl, then lock the outer bowl lid into place.
7. Transfer the outer bowl into the machine, twisting it into place.
8. Press the power button to turn on the unit. Select Scoop. Then select Ice Cream. Let the cycle complete.
9. Lift the Swirl Pint out of the outer bowl.
10. Transfer the ice cream into serving bowls and enjoy immediately.

Per Serving: Calories: 297 | Fat: 17.4g | Sat Fat: 10.7g | Carbohydrates: 33.4g | Fiber: 1g | Sugar: 30.8g | Protein: 3.8g

Walnut Soft Serve

Prep Time: 10 minutes | Serves: 4

Ingredients:

1 cup whole milk
3 tablespoons walnut paste, smooth
1 tablespoon heavy whipped cream
1 teaspoon vanilla extract

Preparation:

1. In a large bowl, merge together all the ingredients until combined.
2. Pour the mixture into an empty Swirl Pint. Snap the lid on the pint and freeze for at least 24 hours.
3. After 24 hours, remove the pint from the freezer and take off the lid. Place the Swirl Pint in the outer bowl, then lock the outer bowl lid into place.
4. Transfer the outer bowl into the machine, twisting it into place.
5. Press the power button to turn on the unit. Select Soft Serve. Then select Ice Cream. Let the cycle complete.
6. Remove the pint from the outer bowl, then attach the soft serve dispensing lid to the pint.
7. Match the blue line on the dispensing lid with the blue line on the dispensing side of the machine, then insert the pint into the machine and twist to lock it into place.
8. Twist the white base of the pint until it is in the "Open" position.
9. Dispense and serve.

Per Serving: Calories: 90 | Fat: 8g | Sat Fat: 3g | Carbohydrates: 8g | Fiber: 0g | Sugar: 5g | Protein: 2g

Chapter 2 Sorbets

Plum Sorbet

Prep Time: 10 minutes | Serves: 4

Ingredients:

3 cups plums, pitted and chopped
3-4 drops liquid stevia

Preparation:

1. In an empty Swirl Pint container, place the plums and stevia and with a potato masher, mash thoroughly.
2. Snap the lid on the pint and freeze for at least 24 hours.
3. After 24 hours, remove the pint from the freezer and take off the lid. Place the Swirl Pint in the outer bowl, then lock the outer bowl lid into place.
4. Transfer the outer bowl into the machine, twisting it into place.
5. Press the power button to turn on the unit. Select Scoop. Then select Sorbet. Let the cycle complete.
6. Lift the Swirl Pint out of the outer bowl.
7. Transfer the sorbet into serving bowls and enjoy immediately.

Per Serving: Calories: 23 | Fat: 0.2g | Sat Fat: 0g | Carbohydrates: 6g | Fiber: 0.7g | Sugar: 5.3g | Protein: 0.4g

Mixed Berries Sorbet

Prep Time: 10 minutes | Serves: 4

Ingredients:

1 pound frozen mixed berries
4¼ ounces caster sugar
1 teaspoon lime juice

Preparation:

1. In a high-powered blender, put in berries and remaining ingredients and process to form a smooth mixture.
2. Pour the mixture into an empty Swirl Pint. Snap the lid on the pint and freeze for at least 24 hours.
3. After 24 hours, remove the pint from the freezer and take off the lid. Place the Swirl Pint in the outer bowl, then lock the outer bowl lid into place.
4. Transfer the outer bowl into the machine, twisting it into place.
5. Press the power button to turn on the unit. Select Scoop. Then select Sorbet. Let the cycle complete.
6. Lift the Swirl Pint out of the outer bowl.
7. Transfer the sorbet into serving bowls and enjoy immediately.

Per Serving: Calories: 178 | Fat: 0.4g | Sat Fat: 0g | Carbohydrates: 44g | Fiber: 4.1g | Sugar: 38.2g | Protein: 0.8g

Lemon Sorbet

Prep Time: 10 minutes | Serves: 4

Ingredients:

1 cup warm water
½ cup granulated sugar
1 tablespoon honey
½ cup lemon juice

Preparation:

1. In a large-sized bowl, put in warm water, sugar and honey and whisk to incorporate thoroughly.
2. Add lemon juice and whisk to incorporate thoroughly.
3. Pour the mixture into an empty Swirl Pint. Snap the lid on the pint and freeze for at least 24 hours.
4. After 24 hours, remove the pint from the freezer and take off the lid. Place the Swirl Pint in the outer bowl, then lock the outer bowl lid into place.
5. Transfer the outer bowl into the machine, twisting it into place.
6. Press the power button to turn on the unit. Select Scoop. Then select Sorbet. Let the cycle complete.
7. Lift the Swirl Pint out of the outer bowl.
8. Transfer the sorbet into serving bowls and enjoy immediately.

Per Serving: Calories: 117 | Fat: 0.2g | Sat Fat: 0.2g | Carbohydrates: 30g | Fiber: 0.1g | Sugar: 30g | Protein: 0.3g

Apricot Sorbet

Prep Time: 40 minutes | Serves: 8

Ingredients:

2 tablespoons lemon juice, freshly squeezed
2 cups apricots, chopped and pitted
1 cup hot water
1 cup sugar, granulated

Preparation:

1. Blitz apricots with all other ingredients in a blender until smooth.
2. Pour the mixture into an empty Swirl Pint. Snap the lid on the pint and freeze for at least 24 hours.
3. After 24 hours, remove the pint from the freezer and take off the lid. Place the Swirl Pint in the outer bowl, then lock the outer bowl lid into place.
4. Transfer the outer bowl into the machine, twisting it into place.
5. Press the power button to turn on the unit. Select Scoop. Then select Sorbet. Let the cycle complete.
6. Lift the Swirl Pint out of the outer bowl.
7. Transfer the sorbet into serving bowls and enjoy immediately.

Per Serving: Calories: 116 | Fat: 1g | Sat Fat: 1g | Carbohydrates: 30g | Fiber: 1g | Sugar: 29g | Protein: 1g

Cherry and Pomegranate Sorbet

Prep Time: 15 minutes | Serves: 3

Ingredients:

½ cup pomegranate juice
1 can cherries

Preparation:

1. In a Ninja Swirl pint, move the cherries and juice and fasten the container with a lid.
2. Freeze the pint for 24 hours.
3. After 24 hours, remove the pint from the freezer and take off the lid. Place the Swirl Pint in the outer bowl, then lock the outer bowl lid into place.
4. Transfer the outer bowl into the machine, twisting it into place.
5. Press the power button to turn on the unit. Select Scoop. Then select Sorbet. Let the cycle complete.
6. Lift the Swirl Pint out of the outer bowl and enjoy.

Per Serving: Calories: 110 | Fat: 0.5g | Sat Fat: 0g | Carbohydrates: 28g | Fiber: 2.8g | Sugar: 23g | Protein: 1.2g

Orange Sorbet

Prep Time: 10 minutes | Serves: 4

Ingredients:

1 (15-ounce) can mandarin oranges in light syrup
¼ cup granulated sugar

Preparation:

1. In a high-powered blender, put in oranges and sugar and process to form a smooth mixture.
2. Pour the mixture into an empty Swirl Pint. Snap the lid on the pint and freeze for at least 24 hours.
3. After 24 hours, remove the pint from the freezer and take off the lid. Place the Swirl Pint in the outer bowl, then lock the outer bowl lid into place.
4. Transfer the outer bowl into the machine, twisting it into place.
5. Press the power button to turn on the unit. Select Scoop. Then select Sorbet. Let the cycle complete.
6. Lift the Swirl Pint out of the outer bowl and serve.

Per Serving: Calories: 86 | Fat: 0g | Sat Fat: 0g | Carbohydrates: 22.7g | Fiber: 0.7g | Sugar: 21.9g | Protein: 0.7g

Watermelon Sorbet

Prep Time: 10 minutes | Serves: 4

Ingredients:

1⅔ cups seedless watermelon chunks
⅓ cup sweetened condensed milk
1 teaspoon lime juice
Pinch of salt

Preparation:

1. In a high-powered blender, put in watermelon and remaining ingredients and process to form a smooth mixture.
2. Pour the mixture into an empty Swirl Pint. Snap the lid on the pint and freeze for at least 24 hours.
3. After 24 hours, remove the pint from the freezer and take off the lid. Place the Swirl Pint in the outer bowl, then lock the outer bowl lid into place.
4. Transfer the outer bowl into the machine, twisting it into place.
5. Press the power button to turn on the unit. Select Scoop. Then select Sorbet. Let the cycle complete.
6. Lift the Swirl Pint out of the outer bowl and enjoy.

Per Serving: Calories: 101 | Fat: 2.3g | Sat Fat: 1.4g | Carbohydrates: 18.7g | Fiber: 0.3g | Sugar: 17.8g | Protein: 2.4g

Strawberry-Banana Sorbet

Prep Time: 5 minutes | Serves: 4

Ingredients:

1 lb. strawberry-banana frozen fruit
⅓ cup agave nectar
3 tablespoons fresh lemon juice

Preparation:

1. In a blender, blitz all the ingredients until smooth.
2. Pour the mixture into an empty Swirl Pint. Snap the lid on the pint and freeze for at least 24 hours.
3. After 24 hours, remove the pint from the freezer and take off the lid. Place the Swirl Pint in the outer bowl, then lock the outer bowl lid into place.
4. Transfer the outer bowl into the machine, twisting it into place.
5. Press the power button to turn on the unit. Select Scoop. Then select Sorbet. Let the cycle complete.
6. Lift the Swirl Pint out of the outer bowl.
7. Transfer the sorbet into serving bowls and enjoy immediately.

Per Serving: Calories: 122 | Fat: 0.2g | Sat Fat: 0g | Carbohydrates: 32g | Fiber: 2g | Sugar: 25g | Protein: 1g

Mango Sorbet

Prep Time: 10 minutes | Serves: 4

Ingredients:

1½ cups frozen mango chunks
½ cup mango juice
¼ cup whole milk
1 teaspoon vanilla extract

Preparation:

1. In a high-powered blender, put in mango chunks and remaining ingredients and process to form a smooth mixture.
2. Pour the mixture into an empty Swirl Pint. Snap the lid on the pint and freeze for at least 24 hours.
3. After 24 hours, remove the pint from the freezer and take off the lid. Place the Swirl Pint in the outer bowl, then lock the outer bowl lid into place.
4. Transfer the outer bowl into the machine, twisting it into place.
5. Press the power button to turn on the unit. Select Scoop. Then select Sorbet. Let the cycle complete.
6. Lift the Swirl Pint out of the outer bowl and serve.

Per Serving: Calories: 58 | Fat: 0.7g | Sat Fat: 0.3g | Carbohydrates. 12.4g | Fiber: 1g | Sugar: 10g | Protein: 1g

Lime Sorbet

Prep Time: 10 minutes | Serves: 4

Ingredients:

1 cup warm water
½ cup granulated sugar
1 tablespoon light corn syrup
½ cup lime juice

Preparation:

1. In a large-sized bowl, put in warm water, sugar and corn syrup, and whisk to incorporate thoroughly.
2. Add lime juice and whisk to incorporate thoroughly.
3. Transfer the blended mixture into an empty Swirl Pint container.
4. Snap the lid on the pint and freeze for at least 24 hours.
5. After 24 hours, remove the pint from the freezer and take off the lid. Place the Swirl Pint in the outer bowl, then lock the outer bowl lid into place.
6. Transfer the outer bowl into the machine, twisting it into place.
7. Press the power button to turn on the unit. Select Scoop. Then select Sorbet. Let the cycle complete.
8. Lift the Swirl Pint out of the outer bowl and enjoy.

Per Serving: Calories: 114 | Fat: 0.1g | Sat Fat: 0g | Carbohydrates: 30.7g | Fiber: 0.1g | Sugar: 26.7g | Protein: 0.1g

Blueberry Sorbet

Prep Time: 10 minutes | Serves: 4

Ingredients:

4½ cups fresh blueberries
¼ cup granulated sugar
2 teaspoons lemon juice

Preparation:

1. In a high-powered blender, put in blueberries, sugar and lemon juice and process to form a smooth mixture.
2. Pour the mixture into an empty Swirl Pint. Snap the lid on the pint and freeze for at least 24 hours.
3. After 24 hours, remove the pint from the freezer and take off the lid. Place the Swirl Pint in the outer bowl, then lock the outer bowl lid into place.
4. Transfer the outer bowl into the machine, twisting it into place.
5. Press the power button to turn on the unit. Select Scoop. Then select Sorbet. Let the cycle complete.
6. Lift the Swirl Pint out of the outer bowl and serve.

Per Serving: Calories: 141 | Fat: 0.6g | Sat Fat: 0g | Carbohydrates: 36.2g | Fiber: 4g | Sugar: 28.8g | Protein: 1.3g

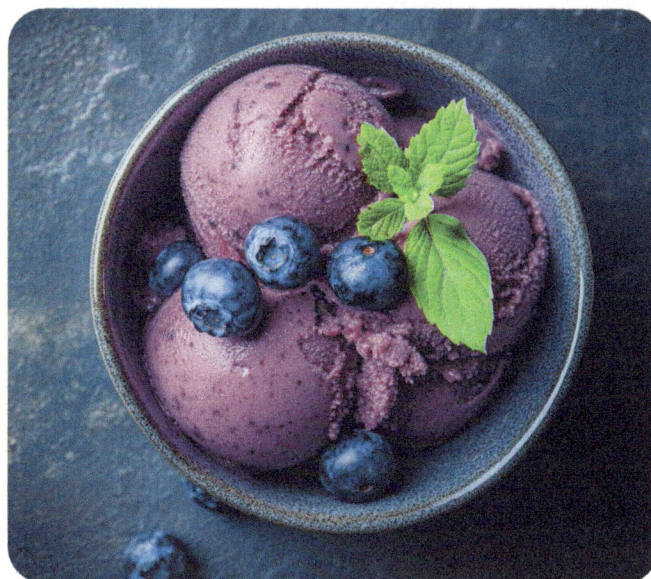

Strawberry Sorbet

Prep Time: 10 minutes | Serves: 4

Ingredients:

3 cups fresh strawberries
⅓ cup water
⅓ cup sugar
¾ cup ginger ale

Preparation:

1. In a high-speed blender, put in strawberries and remaining ingredients and pulse until smooth.
2. Pour the mixture into an empty Swirl Pint. Snap the lid on the pint and freeze for at least 24 hours.
3. After 24 hours, remove the pint from the freezer and take off the lid. Place the Swirl Pint in the outer bowl, then lock the outer bowl lid into place.
4. Transfer the outer bowl into the machine, twisting it into place.
5. Press the power button to turn on the unit. Select Scoop. Then select Sorbet. Let the cycle complete.
6. Lift the Swirl Pint out of the outer bowl.
7. Transfer the sorbet into serving bowls and enjoy immediately.

Per Serving: Calories: 113 | Fat: 0.3g | Sat Fat: 0g | Carbohydrates: 29g | Fiber: 2.2g | Sugar: 25.9g | Protein: 0.7g

Lemony Tropical Fruit Sorbet

Prep Time: 10 minutes | Serves: 4

Ingredients:

1 cup frozen pineapple chunks
1 cup frozen mango chunks
1 cup frozen papaya chunks
½ cup full-fat coconut milk
2 tablespoons honey
2 tablespoons fresh lemon juice
1 teaspoon lemon zest

Preparation:

1. In a high-powered blender, put in mango chunks and remaining ingredients and process to form a smooth mixture.
2. Pour the mixture into an empty Swirl Pint. Snap the lid on the pint and freeze for at least 24 hours.
3. After 24 hours, remove the pint from the freezer and take off the lid. Place the Swirl Pint in the outer bowl, then lock the outer bowl lid into place.
4. Transfer the outer bowl into the machine, twisting it into place.
5. Press the power button to turn on the unit. Select Scoop. Then select Sorbet. Let the cycle complete.
6. Lift the Swirl Pint out of the outer bowl.
7. Transfer the sorbet into serving bowls and enjoy immediately.
Per Serving: Calories: 109 | Fat: 1.8g | Sat Fat: 1.5g | Carbohydrates: 24.6g | Fiber: 2g | Sugar: 21.3g | Protein: 1g

Peach and Tropical Fruit Sorbet

Prep Time: 10 minutes | Serves: 4

Ingredients:

2 cups peaches, peeled, pitted and sliced
2 cup fresh mango, peeled, pitted and sliced
¼ cup pineapple chunks with unsweetened juice
¼ cup fresh orange juice
1 teaspoon maple syrup
½ teaspoon fresh lemon juice

Preparation:

1. In a high-powered blender, put in peaches and remaining ingredients and process to form a smooth mixture.
2. Pour the mixture into an empty Swirl Pint. Snap the lid on the pint and freeze for at least 24 hours.
3. After 24 hours, remove the pint from the freezer and take off the lid. Place the Swirl Pint in the outer bowl, then lock the outer bowl lid into place.
4. Transfer the outer bowl into the machine, twisting it into place.
5. Press the power button to turn on the unit. Select Scoop. Then select Sorbet. Let the cycle complete.
6. Lift the Swirl Pint out of the outer bowl.
7. Transfer the sorbet into serving bowls and enjoy immediately.
Per Serving: Calories: 96 | Fat: 0.6g | Sat Fat: 0.1g | Carbohydrates: 23.5g | Fiber: 2.6g | Sugar: 21.6g | Protein: 1.6g

Pear Sorbet

Prep Time: 10 minutes | Serves: 4

Ingredients:

½ cup sangria seltzer
3 tablespoons maple syrup
1 (15¼-ounce) can pear in a heavy syrup, drained

Preparation:

1. In a large-sized bowl, put in the seltzer and maple syrup and whisk blended thoroughly.
2. In an empty Swirl Pint container, put in the pear pieces and top with agave mixture.
3. Snap the lid on the pint and freeze for at least 24 hours.
3. After 24 hours, remove the pint from the freezer and take off the lid. Place the Swirl Pint in the outer bowl, then lock the outer bowl lid into place.
4. Transfer the outer bowl into the machine, twisting it into place.
5. Press the power button to turn on the unit. Select Scoop. Then select Sorbet. Let the cycle complete.
6. Lift the Swirl Pint out of the outer bowl.
7. Transfer the sorbet into serving bowls and enjoy immediately.
Per Serving: Calories: 126 | Fat: 0.1g | Sat Fat: 0g | Carbohydrates: 30.8g | Fiber: 1.7g | Sugar: 22g | Protein: 0.2g

Basil Pineapple Sorbet

Prep Time: 10 minutes | Serves: 6

Ingredients:

1 lemon juice
1 small piece of ginger, sliced
1 can pineapple chunks
1 lemon zest
1 teaspoon basil leaves
⅓ cup sugar

Preparation:

1. In a blender, blitz all the ingredients until smooth.
2. Pour the mixture into an empty Swirl Pint. Snap the lid on the pint and freeze for at least 24 hours.
3. After 24 hours, remove the pint from the freezer and take off the lid. Place the Swirl Pint in the outer bowl, then lock the outer bowl lid into place.
4. Transfer the outer bowl into the machine, twisting it into place.
5. Press the power button to turn on the unit. Select Scoop. Then select Sorbet. Let the cycle complete.
6. Lift the Swirl Pint out of the outer bowl.
7. Transfer the sorbet into serving bowls and enjoy immediately.
Per Serving: Calories: 34 | Fat: 0.1g | Sat Fat: 0g | Carbohydrates: 8.9g | Fiber: 0.5g | Sugar: 5.9g | Protein: 0.1g

Peach Sorbet

Prep Time: 10 minutes | Serves: 4

Ingredients:

1 (15-ounce) can peaches in light syrup

Preparation:

1. Place the peach pieces into an empty Swirl Pint to the MAX FILL line.
2. Cover the peach pieces with syrup from the can.
3. Snap the lid on the pint and freeze for at least 24 hours.
4. After 24 hours, remove the pint from the freezer and take off the lid. Place the Swirl Pint in the outer bowl, then lock the outer bowl lid into place.
5. Transfer the outer bowl into the machine, twisting it into place.
6. Press the power button to turn on the unit. Select Scoop. Then select Sorbet. Let the cycle complete.
7. Lift the Swirl Pint out of the outer bowl.
8. Transfer the sorbet into serving bowls and enjoy immediately.
Per Serving: Calories: 221 | Fat: 1.5g | Sat Fat: 0g | Carbohydrates: 52.5g | Fiber: 8.6g | Sugar: 52.5g | Protein: 5.3g

Cherry Sorbet

Prep Time: 10 minutes | Serves: 4

Ingredients:

1 pound frozen cherries, pitted
4¼ ounces caster sugar
1 teaspoon lemon juice

Preparation:

1. In a high-powered blender, put in cherries and remaining ingredients and process to form a smooth mixture.
2. Pour the mixture into an empty Swirl Pint. Snap the lid on the pint and freeze for at least 24 hours.
3. After 24 hours, remove the pint from the freezer and take off the lid. Place the Swirl Pint in the outer bowl, then lock the outer bowl lid into place.
4. Transfer the outer bowl into the machine, twisting it into place.
5. Press the power button to turn on the unit. Select Scoop. Then select Sorbet. Let the cycle complete.
6. Lift the Swirl Pint out of the outer bowl and enjoy.
Per Serving: Calories: 165 | Fat: 0.5g | Sat Fat: 0.1g | Carbohydrates: 42.7g | Fiber: 1.8g | Sugar: 40.4g | Protein: 1.1g

Pineapple & Mango Sorbet

Prep Time: 10 minutes | Serves: 4

Ingredients:

1 cup frozen pineapple chunks
½ cup frozen mango chunks
½ cup pineapple mango Juice
¼ cup unsweetened coconut milk
1 teaspoon pure vanilla extract

Preparation:

1. In a high-powered blender, put in pineapple chunks and remaining ingredients and process to form a smooth mixture.
2. Pour the mixture into an empty Swirl Pint. Snap the lid on the pint and freeze for at least 24 hours.
3. After 24 hours, remove the pint from the freezer and take off the lid. Place the Swirl Pint in the outer bowl, then lock the outer bowl lid into place.
4. Transfer the outer bowl into the machine, twisting it into place.
5. Press the power button to turn on the unit. Select Scoop. Then select Sorbet. Let the cycle complete.
6. Lift the Swirl Pint out of the outer bowl and serve.

Per Serving: Calories: 87 | Fat: 3.8g | Sat Fat: 3.2g | Carbohydrates: 13.5g | Fiber: 1.3g | Sugar: 10.6g | Protein: 0.8g

Dill and Basil Sorbet

Prep Time: 15 minutes | Cook Time: 5 minutes | Serves: 4

Ingredients:

½ cup water
¼ cup granulated sugar
2 large fresh dill sprigs, stemmed
2 large fresh basil sprigs, stemmed
1 cup ice water
2 tablespoons fresh lemon juice

Preparation:

1. In a saucepan, merge together sugar and water.
2. Let the sugar get dissolved over medium heat for about 5 minutes.
3. Stir in the dill and basil sprigs and eliminate from the heat.
4. Add ice water and lemon juice and mix well.
5. Pour the mixture into an empty Swirl Pint. Snap the lid on the pint and freeze for at least 24 hours.
6. After 24 hours, remove the pint from the freezer and take off the lid. Place the Swirl Pint in the outer bowl, then lock the outer bowl lid into place.
7. Transfer the outer bowl into the machine, twisting it into place.
8. Press the power button to turn on the unit. Select Scoop. Then select Sorbet. Let the cycle complete.
9. Lift the Swirl Pint out of the outer bowl.
10. Transfer the sorbet into serving bowls and enjoy immediately.

Per Serving: Calories: 51 | Fat: 0.1g | Sat Fat: 0g.1 | Carbohydrates: 13.1g | Fiber: 0.1g | Sugar: 12.7g | Protein: 0.2g

Pineapple, Mango and Banana Sorbet

Prep Time: 5 minutes | Serves: 2

Ingredients:

¾ cup ripe pineapple, cut into ½-inch pieces
1 ripe banana, cut into ½-inch slices
1¼ mangoes, peeled, cut into ½-inch pieces

Preparation:

1. In a Ninja Swirl pint, move the mangoes along with the pineapples and bananas, and fasten the container with a lid.
2. Freeze the pint for 24 hours.
3. After 24 hours, open the pint, fix it into the outer bowl of Ninja Swirl, then lock the outer bowl lid into place.
4. Transfer the outer bowl into the machine, twisting it into place.
5. Press the power button to turn on the unit. Select Scoop. Then select Sorbet. Let the cycle complete.
6. Lift the Swirl Pint out of the outer bowl and enjoy.

Per Serving: Calories: 203 | Fat: 0.6g | Sat Fat: 0.2g | Carbohydrates: 52g | Fiber: 7.6g | Sugar: 34g | Protein: 3g

Rhubarb Sorbet

Prep Time: 10 minutes | Serves: 6

Ingredients:

3 cups rhubarb, chopped
3 drops vanilla essence
3 tablespoons liquid glucose
1 lemon juice
⅔ cup golden caster sugar
2 teaspoons star anise

Preparation:

1. In a blender, blitz all the ingredients until smooth.
2. Pour the mixture into an empty Swirl Pint. Snap the lid on the pint and freeze for at least 24 hours.
3. After 24 hours, remove the pint from the freezer and take off the lid. Place the Swirl Pint in the outer bowl, then lock the outer bowl lid into place.
4. Transfer the outer bowl into the machine, twisting it into place.
5. Press the power button to turn on the unit. Select Scoop. Then select Sorbet. Let the cycle complete.
6. Lift the Swirl Pint out of the outer bowl.
7. Transfer the sorbet into serving bowls and enjoy immediately.

Per Serving: Calories: 17 | Fat: 0.2g | Sat Fat: 0g | Carbohydrates: 3.6g | Fiber: 1.2g | Sugar: 1.1g | Protein: 0.7g

Banana Sorbet

Prep Time: 5 minutes | Serves: 4

Ingredients:

4 large bananas
Water, as required

Preparation:

1. In a blender, blitz all the ingredients until smooth.
2. Pour the mixture into an empty Swirl Pint. Snap the lid on the pint and freeze for at least 24 hours.
3. After 24 hours, remove the pint from the freezer and take off the lid. Place the Swirl Pint in the outer bowl, then lock the outer bowl lid into place.
4. Transfer the outer bowl into the machine, twisting it into place.
5. Press the power button to turn on the unit. Select Scoop. Then select Sorbet. Let the cycle complete.
6. Lift the Swirl Pint out of the outer bowl.
7. Transfer the sorbet into serving bowls and enjoy immediately.

Per Serving: Calories: 61 | Fat: 0.2g | Sat Fat: 0.1g | Carbohydrates: 15.5g | Fiber: 1.8g | Sugar: 8.3g | Protein: 0.7g

Raspberry Sorbet

Prep Time: 10 minutes | Serves: 4

Ingredients:

4½ cups fresh raspberries
¼ cup granulated sugar
2 teaspoons lime juice

Preparation:

1. In a high-powered blender, put in raspberries, sugar and lime juice and process to form a smooth mixture.
2. Pour the mixture into an empty Swirl Pint. Snap the lid on the pint and freeze for at least 24 hours.
3. After 24 hours, remove the pint from the freezer and take off the lid. Place the Swirl Pint in the outer bowl, then lock the outer bowl lid into place.
4. Transfer the outer bowl into the machine, twisting it into place.
5. Press the power button to turn on the unit. Select Scoop. Then select Sorbet. Let the cycle complete.
6. Lift the Swirl Pint out of the outer bowl.
7. Transfer the sorbet into serving bowls and enjoy immediately.

Per Serving: Calories: 119 | Fat: 0.9g | Sat Fat: 0g | Carbohydrates: 29.2g | Fiber: 9g | Sugar: 18.7g | Protein: 1.7g

Grape Sorbet

Ingredients:

1½ cups water
¾ cup grape juice concentrate, frozen
1 tablespoon lemon juice

Preparation:

1. In a bowl, merge the grape juice concentrate with lemon juice and water.
2. Pour the mixture into an empty Swirl Pint. Snap the lid on the pint and freeze for at least 24 hours.
3. After 24 hours, remove the pint from the freezer and take off the lid. Place the Swirl Pint in the outer bowl, then lock the outer bowl lid into place.
4. Transfer the outer bowl into the machine, twisting it into place.
5. Press the power button to turn on the unit. Select Scoop. Then select Sorbet. Let the cycle complete.
6. Lift the Swirl Pint out of the outer bowl.
7. Transfer the sorbet into serving bowls and enjoy immediately.

Per Serving: Calories: 25 | Fat: 0.1g | Sat Fat: 0g | Carbohydrates: 6g | Fiber: 0.1g | Sugar: 6g | Protein: 0.1g

Chapter 3 Milkshakes

Chocolate Banana Milkshake

Prep Time: 5 minutes | Cook Time: 0 minute | Serves: 2

Ingredients:

½ cup cashew milk
1½ cups vegan chocolate ice cream
½ cup fresh banana, ripe
1 tablespoon coffee powder, instant

Preparation:

1. Move the ice cream into a Ninja Swirl pint container.
2. Use a spoon to make a hole that is 1½ inches wide in the pint's bottom.
3. Add the remaining ingredients to the hole.
4. Place the Swirl Pint in the outer bowl of Ninja Swirl, then lock the outer bowl lid into place.
5. Transfer the outer bowl into the machine, twisting it into place.
6. Press the power button to turn on the unit. Select Scoop. Then select Milkshake. Let the cycle complete.
7. Lift the Swirl Pint out of the outer bowl.
8. Ladle out the shake into serving glasses and serve chilled.
Per Serving: Calories: 142 | Fat: 5.9g | Sat Fat: 3.4g | Carbohydrates: 20g | Fiber: 1g | Sugar: 15g | Protein: 2g

Pistachio Milkshake

Prep Time: 10 minutes | Serves: 2

Ingredients:

1½ cups vanilla ice cream
½ cup whole milk
2 tablespoons maple syrup
¼ cup pistachios, chopped
¼ teaspoon vanilla extract

Preparation:

1. In an empty Ninja Swirl pint container, put in ice cream, followed by milk, maple syrup, pistachios and vanilla extract.
2. Place the Swirl Pint in the outer bowl of Ninja Swirl, then lock the outer bowl lid into place.
3. Transfer the outer bowl into the machine, twisting it into place.
4. Press the power button to turn on the unit. Select Scoop. Then select Milkshake. Let the cycle complete.
5. Lift the Swirl Pint out of the outer bowl.
6. Transfer the shake into serving glasses and enjoy immediately.
Per Serving: Calories: 233 | Fat: 10.8g | Sat Fat: 4.9g | Carbohydrates: 30.3g | Fiber: 1.1g | Sugar: 26.2g | Protein: 5.2g

Berries Milkshake

Prep Time: 10 minutes | Serves: 2

Ingredients:

½ cup milk
1½ cups vanilla ice cream
½ cup fresh mixed berries

Preparation:

1. Move the ice cream, milk, and berries into a Ninja Swirl pint container.
2. Snap the lid on the pint and freeze for at least 8 hours.
3. After 8 hours, remove the pint from the freezer and take off the lid. Place the Swirl Pint in the outer bowl, then lock the outer bowl lid into place.
4. Transfer the outer bowl into the machine, twisting it into place.
5. Press the power button to turn on the unit. Select Scoop. Then select Milkshake. Let the cycle complete.
6. Lift the Swirl Pint out of the outer bowl.
7. Ladle out the shake into serving glasses and serve chilled.
Per Serving: Calories: 153 | Fat: 6.6g | Sat Fat: 4.1g | Carbohydrates: 19.3g | Fiber: 1.6g | Sugar: 15.8g | Protein: 4g

Chocolate Cookies Milkshake

Prep Time: 10 minutes | Serves: 2

Ingredients:

1 cup chocolate ice cream
1 cup milk
2 small chocolate cookies, crushed

Preparation:

1. In an empty Ninja Swirl pint container, put in the ice cream.
2. With a spoon, create a 1½-inch wide hole in the center that reaches the bottom of the Swirl pint container.
3. Put in remaining ingredients into the hole.
4. Place the Swirl Pint in the outer bowl, then lock the outer bowl lid into place.
5. Transfer the outer bowl into the machine, twisting it into place.
6. Press the power button to turn on the unit. Select Scoop. Then select Milkshake. Let the cycle complete.
7. Lift the Swirl Pint out of the outer bowl.
8. Transfer the shake into serving glasses and enjoy immediately.
Per Serving: Calories: 189 | Fat: 7.4g | Sat Fat: 4g | Carbohydrates: 24.8g | Fiber: 0.6g | Sugar: 16.9g | Protein: 6.1g

Strawberry Vanilla Milkshake

Prep Time: 10 minutes | Serves: 3

Ingredients:

2 cups strawberry ice cream
1 cup coconut milk
1 teaspoon vanilla extract

Preparation:

1. In an empty Ninja Swirl pint, put in the ice cream.
2. Top with the coconut milk and vanilla extract and lightly blend to incorporate.
3. Arrange the container into the outer bowl of Ninja Swirl, then lock the outer bowl lid into place.
4. Transfer the outer bowl into the machine, twisting it into place.
5. Press the power button to turn on the unit. Select Scoop. Then select Milkshake. Let the cycle complete.
6. Lift the Swirl Pint out of the outer bowl.
7. Transfer the shake into serving glasses and enjoy immediately.
Per Serving: Calories: 215 | Fat: 15.7g | Sat Fat: 13g | Carbohydrates: 12.9g | Fiber: 0.3g | Sugar: 11.5g | Protein: 2.5g

Pumpkin Latte Milkshake

Prep Time: 10 minutes | Cook Time: 5 minutes | Serves: 4

Ingredients:

2 cups whole milk
2 tablespoons sugar, granulated
1 cup coffee, brewed
4 cups vanilla ice cream
½ cup pumpkin puree, canned
1 teaspoon pumpkin pie spice
2 teaspoons vanilla extract

Preparation:

1. In a saucepan, lightly boil the milk and then ladle out in a mixing bowl.
2. Merge in the pumpkin puree, pumpkin pie spice, sugar, coffee, and vanilla extract.
3. Whisk well and refrigerate for 1 hour.
4. Transfer the mixture and vanilla ice cream into an empty Swirl Pint. Snap the lid on the pint and freeze for 24 hours.
5. After 24 hours, remove the pint from the freezer and take off the lid. Place the Swirl Pint in the outer bowl, then lock the outer bowl lid into place.
6. Transfer the outer bowl into the machine, twisting it into place.
7. Press the power button to turn on the unit. Select Scoop. Then select Milkshake. Let the cycle complete.
8. Lift the Swirl Pint out of the outer bowl.
9. Ladle out the shake into serving glasses and serve chilled.
Per Serving: Calories: 260 | Fat: 11g | Sat Fat: 6g | Carbohydrates: 30g | Fiber: 1g | Sugar:27 g | Protein: 6 g

Blueberry Vanilla Milkshake

Prep Time: 10 minutes | Serves: 2

Ingredients:

1½ ounces vanilla ice cream
5¼ ounces fresh blueberries
3 ounces full-fat coconut milk
Dash of vanilla extract

Preparation:

1. In an empty Ninja Swirl pint container, put in the ice cream.
2. Top with the blueberries, coconut milk and vanilla extract and lightly blend to incorporate.
3. Place the Swirl Pint in the outer bowl, then lock the outer bowl lid into place.
4. Transfer the outer bowl into the machine, twisting it into place.
5. Press the power button to turn on the unit. Select Scoop. Then select Milkshake. Let the cycle complete.
6. Lift the Swirl Pint out of the outer bowl and enjoy.

Per Serving: Calories: 310 | Fat: 22g | Sat Fat: 19.9g | Carbohydrates: 24.3g | Fiber: 2.2g | Sugar: 17.9g | Protein: 3.8g

Vanilla Shortbread Cookies Milkshake

Prep Time: 10 minutes | Serves: 2

Ingredients:

2 cups vanilla ice cream
½ cup whole milk
¼ cup shortbread cookies, broken
2 tablespoons cookie butter

Preparation:

1. In an empty Ninja Swirl pint container, put in the ice cream.
2. With a spoon, create a 1½-inch wide hole in the center that reaches the bottom of the Swirl pint container.
3. Put in remaining ingredients into the hole.
4. Arrange the container into the outer bowl of Ninja Swirl, then lock the outer bowl lid into place.
5. Transfer the outer bowl into the machine, twisting it into place.
6. Press the power button to turn on the unit. Select Scoop. Then select Milkshake. Let the cycle complete.
7. Lift the Swirl Pint out of the outer bowl.
8. Transfer the shake into serving glasses and enjoy immediately.

Per Serving: Calories: 322 | Fat: 22.4g | Sat Fat: 13.3g | Carbohydrates: 25.9g | Fiber: 0.8g | Sugar: 21.3g | Protein: 4.9g

Cherry Milkshake

Prep Time: 5 minutes | Serves: 2

Ingredients:

3 scoops vanilla ice cream, softened
¼ cup milk, chilled
1 cup cherries, pitted and halved

Preparation:

1. Move all the ingredients into a Ninja Swirl pint container.
2. Snap the lid on the pint and freeze for at least 8 hours.
3. After 8 hours, remove the pint from the freezer and take off the lid. Place the Swirl Pint in the outer bowl, then lock the outer bowl lid into place.
4. Transfer the outer bowl into the machine, twisting it into place.
5. Press the power button to turn on the unit. Select Scoop. Then select Milkshake. Let the cycle complete.
6. Lift the Swirl Pint out of the outer bowl.
7. Ladle out the shake into serving glasses and serve chilled.

Per Serving: Calories: 130 | Fat: 2g | Sat Fat: 1g | Carbohydrates: 25g | Fiber: 2g | Sugar: 21g | Protein: 3g

Strawberry Marshmallow Milkshake

Prep Time: 10 minutes | Serves: 2

Ingredients:

1½ cups strawberry ice cream
½ cup whole milk
1 tablespoon marshmallow topping

Preparation:

1. In an empty Ninja Swirl pint, put in the ice cream.
2. With a spoon, create a 1½-inch wide hole in the center that reaches the bottom of the Swirl pint container.
3. Put in remaining ingredients into the hole.
4. Place the Swirl Pint in the outer bowl, then lock the outer bowl lid into place.
5. Transfer the outer bowl into the machine, twisting it into place.
6. Press the power button to turn on the unit. Select Scoop. Then select Milkshake. Let the cycle complete.
7. Lift the Swirl Pint out of the outer bowl.
8. Transfer the shake into serving glasses and enjoy immediately.

Per Serving: Calories: 172 | Fat: 7.3g | Sat Fat: 4.5g | Carbohydrates: 22.7g | Fiber: 0.4g | Sugar: 18.4g | Protein: 3.8g

Coffee Milkshake

Prep Time: 10 minutes | Serves: 2

Ingredients:

1½ cups coffee ice cream
½ cup milk
2 tablespoons sweetened condensed milk
¼ teaspoon salt

Preparation:

1. In an empty Ninja Swirl pint container, put in the ice cream.
2. Top with the remaining ingredients and gently blend to incorporate.
3. Arrange the container into the outer bowl of Ninja Swirl, then lock the outer bowl lid into place.
4. Transfer the outer bowl into the machine, twisting it into place.
5. Press the power button to turn on the unit. Select Scoop. Then select Milkshake. Let the cycle complete.
6. Lift the Swirl Pint out of the outer bowl.
7. Transfer the shake into serving glasses and enjoy immediately.

Per Serving: Calories: 1954 | Fat: 8.2g | Sat Fat: 5.2g | Carbohydrates: 25.4g | Fiber: 0.4g | Sugar: 23.6g | Protein: 5.2g

Chocolate and Sandwich Cookie Milkshake

Prep Time: 10 minutes | Serves: 2

Ingredients:

1½ cups chocolate ice cream
½ cup whole milk
2 tablespoons cream cheese, softened
3 chocolate sandwich cookies, crushed

Preparation:

1. In an empty Ninja Swirl pint container, put in ice cream and remaining ingredients and blend to incorporate.
2. Snap the lid on the pint and freeze for at least 8 hours.
3. After 8 hours, remove the pint from the freezer and take off the lid. Place the Swirl Pint in the outer bowl, then lock the outer bowl lid into place.
4. Transfer the outer bowl into the machine, twisting it into place.
5. Press the power button to turn on the unit. Select Scoop. Then select Milkshake. Let the cycle complete.
6. Lift the Swirl Pint out of the outer bowl.
7. Transfer the shake into serving glasses and serve immediately.

Per Serving: Calories: 339 | Fat: 18.2g | Sat Fat: 8.2g | Carbohydrates: 42g | Fiber: 0.4g | Sugar: 13.7g | Protein: 6g

Caramel Pretzel Milkshake

Prep Time: 2 minutes | Serves: 2

Ingredients:

½ cup whole milk
⅓ pretzels, broken
1½ cups vanilla ice cream
2 tablespoons caramel sauce
2 pinches sea salt

Preparation:

1. Move the ice cream into a Ninja Swirl pint container.
2. Use a spoon to make a hole that is 1½ inches wide in the pint's bottom.
3. Add the remaining ingredients to the hole.
4. Snap the lid on the pint and freeze for at least 8 hours.
5. After 8 hours, remove the pint from the freezer and take off the lid. Place the Swirl Pint in the outer bowl, then lock the outer bowl lid into place.
6. Transfer the outer bowl into the machine, twisting it into place.
7. Press the power button to turn on the unit. Select Scoop. Then select Milkshake. Let the cycle complete.
8. Lift the Swirl Pint out of the outer bowl.
9. Ladle out the shake into serving glasses and serve chilled.
Per Serving: Calories: 193 | Fat: 7g | Sat Fat: 4g | Carbohydrates: 23g | Fiber: 0.5g | Sugar: 13g | Protein: 4g

Cinnamon Almond Milkshake

Prep Time: 10 minutes | Serves: 2

Ingredients:

1½ cups vanilla ice cream
½ cup whole milk
2 tablespoons honey
¼ cup almonds, chopped
¼ teaspoon ground cinnamon
Pinch of ground cardamom

Preparation:

1. In an empty Ninja Swirl pint container, put in ice cream, followed by milk, honey, almonds, cinnamon and cardamom.
2. Place the Swirl Pint in the outer bowl of Ninja Swirl, then lock the outer bowl lid into place.
3. Transfer the outer bowl into the machine, twisting it into place.
4. Press the power button to turn on the unit. Select Scoop. Then select Milkshake. Let the cycle complete.
5. Lift the Swirl Pint out of the outer bowl.
6. Transfer the shake into serving glasses and enjoy immediately.
Per Serving: Calories: 273 | Fat: 13.2g | Sat Fat: 5g | Carbohydrates: 34.9g | Fiber: 2.1g | Sugar: 31.5g | Protein: 6.3g

Oreo Milkshake

Prep Time: 10 minutes | Serves: 2

Ingredients:

1½ cups vanilla ice cream
3 Oreo cookies
¼ cup whole milk

Preparation:

1. In an empty Ninja Swirl pint container, put in ice cream, followed by cookies and milk.
2. Arrange the container into the outer bowl of Ninja Swirl, then lock the outer bowl lid into place.
3. Transfer the outer bowl into the machine, twisting it into place.
4. Press the power button to turn on the unit. Select Scoop. Then select Milkshake.
5. Once the program finishes, rotate the outer bowl and detach it from the machine.
6. Transfer the shake into serving glasses and enjoy immediately.
Per Serving: Calories: 191 | Fat: 9.1g | Sat Fat: 4.5g | Carbohydrates: 24.1g | Fiber: 0.8g | Sugar: 18.2g | Protein: 3.5g

Rainbow Vanilla Milkshake

Prep Time: 2 minutes | Serves: 2

Ingredients:

2 cups vegan French vanilla coffee creamer
1 tablespoon raw agave nectar
2-ounces vanilla vodka
1 tablespoon rainbow sprinkles

Preparation:

1. Move all the ingredients into a Ninja Swirl pint container.
2. Snap the lid on the pint and freeze for 24 hours.
3. After 24 hours, open the pint, fix it into the outer bowl of Ninja Swirl, then lock the outer bowl lid into place.
4. Transfer the outer bowl into the machine, twisting it into place.
5. Press the power button to turn on the unit. Select Scoop. Then select Milkshake. Let the cycle complete.
6. Lift the Swirl Pint out of the outer bowl and enjoy.
Per Serving: Calories: 541 | Fat: 34g | Sat Fat: 18g | Carbohydrates: 6g | Fiber: 0g | Sugar: 2g | Protein: 5g

Mint Cookie Milkshake

Prep Time: 5 minutes | Serves: 4

Ingredients:

3 cream cookies
1½ cups mint ice cream
¼ cup milk

Preparation:

1. Move all the ingredients into a Ninja Swirl pint container.
2. Snap the lid on the pint and freeze for at least 8 hours.
3. After 8 hours, remove the pint from the freezer and take off the lid. Place the Swirl Pint in the outer bowl, then lock the outer bowl lid into place.
4. Transfer the outer bowl into the machine, twisting it into place.
5. Press the power button to turn on the unit. Select Scoop. Then select Milkshake. Let the cycle complete.
6. Lift the Swirl Pint out of the outer bowl.
7. Ladle out the shake into serving glasses and serve chilled.

Per Serving: Calories: 113 | Fat: 2g | Sat Fat: 0.8g | Carbohydrates: 21g | Fiber: 0.6g | Sugar: 6.7g | Protein: 3g

Chocolate Chip and Almond Milkshake

Prep Time: 10 minutes | Serves: 2

Ingredients:

1½ cups leche ice cream
½ cup unsweetened almond milk
2 tablespoons roasted almonds, cut up
2 tablespoons chocolate chips
2 tablespoons shredded coconut

Preparation:

1. In an empty Ninja Swirl pint, put in the ice cream.
2. Top with the remaining ingredients and gently blend to incorporate.
3. Arrange the container into the outer bowl of Ninja Swirl, then lock the outer bowl lid into place.
4. Transfer the outer bowl into the machine, twisting it into place.
5. Press the power button to turn on the unit. Select Scoop. Then select Milkshake. Let the cycle complete.
6. Lift the Swirl Pint out of the outer bowl.
7. Transfer the shake into serving glasses and enjoy immediately.

Per Serving: Calories: 231 | Fat: 13.9g | Sat Fat: 7g | Carbohydrates: 23.8g | Fiber: 1.8g | Sugar: 20.2g | Protein: 4.7g

Vanilla Marshmallow Milkshake

Prep Time: 10 minutes | Serves: 2

)Ingredients:

1½ cups vanilla ice cream
½ cup coconut milk
1 tablespoon marshmallow topping

)Preparation:

1. Place ice cream and milk in an empty Swirl Pint.
2. Arrange the container into the outer bowl of Ninja Swirl, then lock the outer bowl lid into place.
3. Transfer the outer bowl into the machine, twisting it into place.
4. Press the power button to turn on the unit. Select Scoop. Then select Milkshake. Let the cycle complete.
5. Lift the Swirl Pint out of the outer bowl.
6. Transfer the shake into serving glasses and sprinkle with marshmallow topping. Enjoy immediately.

Per Serving: Calories: 243 | Fat: 19.6g | Sat Fat: 16.1g | Carbohydrates: 20.8g | Fiber: 1.7g | Sugar: 17g | Protein: 3.1g

Mango Milkshake

Prep Time: 10 minutes | Serves: 2

)Ingredients:

1½ cups mango ice cream
½ cup full-fat coconut milk

)Preparation:

1. In an empty Ninja Swirl pint container, put in mango ice cream, followed by coconut milk.
2. Arrange the container into the outer bowl of Ninja Swirl, then lock the outer bowl lid into place.
3. Transfer the outer bowl into the machine, twisting it into place.
4. Press the power button to turn on the unit. Select Scoop. Then select Milkshake. Let the cycle complete.
5. Lift the Swirl Pint out of the outer bowl.
6. Transfer the shake into serving glasses and enjoy immediately.

Per Serving: Calories: 223 | Fat: 17.2g | Sat Fat: 14.4g | Carbohydrates: 14g | Fiber: 0.4g | Sugar: 11.5g | Protein: 2.7g

Chocolate Yogurt Milkshake

Prep Time: 10 minutes | Serves: 2

Ingredients:

1 scoop chocolate whey protein powder
1 cup frozen chocolate yogurt
1 cup whole milk

Preparation:

1. Move the yogurt, protein powder, and milk into a Ninja Swirl pint container.
2. Snap the lid on the pint and freeze for at least 8 hours.
3. After 8 hours, remove the pint from the freezer and take off the lid. Place the Swirl Pint in the outer bowl, then lock the outer bowl lid into place.
4. Transfer the outer bowl into the machine, twisting it into place.
5. Press the power button to turn on the unit. Select Scoop. Then select Milkshake. Let the cycle complete.
6. Lift the Swirl Pint out of the outer bowl.
7. Ladle out the shake into serving glasses and serve chilled.

Per Serving: Calories: 242 | Fat: 4.8g | Sat Fat: 2.8g | Carbohydrates: 30.7g | Fiber: 0.4g | Sugar: 27.5g | Protein: 18.6g

Strawberry Ice Cream Milkshake

Prep Time: 10 minutes | Serves: 2

Ingredients:

1½ cups strawberry ice cream
½ cup whole milk

Preparation:

1. In an empty Ninja Swirl pint container, put in ice cream, followed by milk.
2. Arrange the container into the outer bowl of Ninja Swirl, then lock the outer bowl lid into place.
3. Transfer the outer bowl into the machine, twisting it into place.
4. Press the power button to turn on the unit. Select Scoop. Then select Milkshake. Let the cycle complete.
5. Lift the Swirl Pint out of the outer bowl.
6. Transfer the shake into serving glasses and enjoy immediately.

Per Serving: Calories: 139 | Fat: 7.2g | Sat Fat: 4.5g | Carbohydrates: 14.8g | Fiber: 0.4g | Sugar: 13.7g | Protein: 3.7g

Chocolate Hazelnut Milkshake

Prep Time: 10 minutes | Serves: 2

Ingredients:

1½ cups chocolate ice cream
½ cup whole milk
¼ cup hazelnut spread

Preparation:

1. In an empty Ninja Swirl pint container, put in the ice cream.
2. Top with the remaining ingredients and gently blend to incorporate.
3. Arrange the container into the outer bowl of Ninja Swirl, then lock the outer bowl lid into place.
4. Transfer the outer bowl into the machine, twisting it into place.
5. Press the power button to turn on the unit. Select Scoop. Then select Milkshake. Let the cycle complete.
6. Lift the Swirl Pint out of the outer bowl.
7. Transfer the shake into serving glasses and enjoy immediately.

Per Serving: Calories: 329 | Fat: 19.2g | Sat Fat: 7.7g | Carbohydrates: 34.8g | Fiber: 1.4g | Sugar: 32.7g | Protein: 5.9g

Apple Pie Milkshake

Prep Time: 10 minutes | Serves: 2

Ingredients:

1½ cups vanilla ice cream
2 ounces premade apple pie
¼ cup whole milk

Preparation:

1. In an empty Ninja Swirl pint container, put in the ice cream.
2. With a spoon, create a 1½-inch wide hole in the center that reaches the bottom of the Swirl pint container.
3. Put in remaining ingredients into the hole.
4. Arrange the container into the outer bowl of Ninja Swirl, then lock the outer bowl lid into place.
5. Transfer the outer bowl into the machine, twisting it into place.
6. Press the power button to turn on the unit. Select Scoop. Then select Milkshake. Let the cycle complete.
7. Lift the Swirl Pint out of the outer bowl.
8. Transfer the shake into serving glasses and enjoy immediately.

Per Serving: Calories: 191 | Fat: 9.6g | Sat Fat: 4.6g | Carbohydrates: 22.7g | Fiber: 0.7g | Sugar: 16.1g | Protein: 3.2g

Chai Tea Coconut Milk Milkshake

Prep Time: 10 minutes | Cook Time: 5 minutes | Serves: 2

Ingredients:

½ cup coconut milk
2 chai tea bags
1½ cups vanilla coconut milk ice cream

Preparation:

1. In a small saucepan, put in coconut milk on burner at around medium heat and cook until boiling.
2. Take off from burner and add in the chai tea bags.
3. Cover the pan and let it steep until cooled thoroughly.
4. After cooling, squeeze the tea bags into the milk.
5. Then discard the tea bags.
6. In an empty Ninja Swirl pint container, put in the ice cream.
7. With a spoon, create a 1½-inch wide hole in the center that reaches the bottom of the Swirl pint container.
8. Add the chai coconut milk into the hole.
9. Arrange the container into the outer bowl of Ninja Swirl, then lock the outer bowl lid into place.
10. Transfer the outer bowl into the machine, twisting it into place.
11. Press the power button to turn on the unit. Select Scoop. Then select Milkshake. Let the cycle complete.
12. Lift the Swirl Pint out of the outer bowl.
13. Transfer the shake into serving glasses and enjoy immediately.
Per Serving: Calories: 241 | Fat: 19.6g | Sat Fat: 16.1g | Carbohydrates: 15.3g | Fiber: 1.7g | Sugar: 12.5g | Protein: 3.1g

Cinnamon Pecan Milkshake

Prep Time: 10 minutes | Serves: 2

Ingredients:

1½ cups vanilla ice cream
2 tablespoons maple syrup
¼ cup pecans, chopped
Pinch of salt
½ cup soy milk, unsweetened
1 teaspoon ground cinnamon

Preparation:

1. Move the ice cream, soy milk, maple syrup, pecans, cinnamon and salt into a Ninja Swirl pint container.
2. Snap the lid on the pint and freeze for at least 8 hours.
3. After 8 hours, remove the pint from the freezer and take off the lid. Place the Swirl Pint in the outer bowl, then lock the outer bowl lid into place.
4. Transfer the outer bowl into the machine, twisting it into place.
5. Press the power button to turn on the unit. Select Scoop. Then select Milkshake. Let the cycle complete.
6. Lift the Swirl Pint out of the outer bowl and enjoy.
Per Serving: Calories: 309 | Fat: 18.5g | Sat Fat: 4.7g | Carbohydrates: 32.6g | Fiber: 3.2g | Sugar: 25.5g | Protein: 5.6g

Cherry and Chocolate Chip Ice Cream

Prep Time: 15 minutes | Serves: 4

Ingredients:

½ cup frozen cherries, thawed and squeezed
½ cup granulated sugar
1 cup whole milk
½ teaspoon vanilla extract
½ teaspoon strawberry extract
⅓ cup heavy cream
⅓ cup chocolate chips

Preparation:

1. In a high-powered blender, put in cherries and remaining ingredients except for chocolate chips and process to form a smooth mixture.
2. Transfer the blended mixture into an empty Ninja Swirl pint container.
3. Put in heavy cream and blend to incorporate.
4. Snap the lid on the pint and freeze for at least 24 hours.
5. After 24 hours, remove the pint from the freezer and take off the lid. Place the Swirl Pint in the outer bowl, then lock the outer bowl lid into place.
6. Transfer the outer bowl into the machine, twisting it into place.
7. Press the power button to turn on the unit. Select Scoop. Then select Ice Cream.
8. When the program is completed, use a spoon to create a 1½-inch (4 cm) wide hole that reaches the bottom of the processed portion of the Swirl Pint. Add chocolate chips to the hole in the Swirl Pint and press "MIX-IN" button.
9. Once the program finishes, rotate the outer bowl and detach it from the machine.
10. Transfer the ice cream into serving bowls and enjoy immediately.
Per Serving: Calories: 250 | Fat: 9.9g | Sat Fat: 6.4g | Carbohydrates: 38.6g | Fiber: 0.8g | Sugar: 37.3g | Protein: 3.4g

Strawberry Banana Ice Cream

Prep Time: 10 minutes | Serves: 4

Ingredients:

1 (11.5 ounce) bottle strawberry protein shake
1 small banana, peel removed
2 fresh whole strawberries
½ cup fresh strawberries, cut up

Preparation:

1. In a high-powered blender, put in protein shake, banana and 2 strawberries and process to form a smooth mixture.
2. Transfer the mixture into an empty Swirl Pint. Snap the lid on the pint and freeze for at least 24 hours.
3. After 24 hours, remove the pint from the freezer and take off the lid. Place the Swirl Pint in the outer bowl, then lock the outer bowl lid into place.
4. Transfer the outer bowl into the machine, twisting it into place.
5. Press the power button to turn on the unit. Select Scoop. Then select Ice Cream.
6. When the program is completed, use a spoon to create a 1½-inch (4 cm) wide hole that reaches the bottom of the processed portion of the Swirl Pint. Add cut up strawberries to the hole in the Swirl Pint and press "MIX-IN" button.
7. Once the program finishes, rotate the outer bowl and detach it from the machine.
8. Transfer the ice cream into serving bowls and enjoy immediately.
Per Serving: Calories: 31 | Fat: 2.5g | Sat Fat: 0g | Carbohydrates: 46.7g | Fiber: 3.4g | Sugar: 36.6g | Protein: 35.3g

Peanut Butter Ice Cream

Prep Time: 10 minutes | Cook Time: 10 seconds | Serves: 4

Ingredients:

1 tablespoon cream cheese
⅓ cup granulated sugar
1 teaspoon vanilla extract
¾ cup heavy cream
1 cup whole milk
¼ cup peanut butter chips

Preparation:

1. In a large-sized, microwave-safe bowl, put in cream cheese and microwave for 10 seconds.
2. Put in sugar and vanilla extract and whisk to form a frosting mixture.
3. Slowly put in the heavy cream and milk and whisk to incorporate thoroughly.
4. Pour the mixture into an empty Swirl Pint. Snap the lid on the pint and freeze for at least 24 hours.
5. After 24 hours, remove the pint from the freezer and take off the lid. Place the Swirl Pint in the outer bowl, then lock the outer bowl lid into place.
6. Transfer the outer bowl into the machine, twisting it into place.
7. Press the power button to turn on the unit. Select Scoop. Then select Ice Cream.
8. When the program is completed, use a spoon to create a 1½-inch (4 cm) wide hole that reaches the bottom of the processed portion of the Swirl Pint. Add peanut butter chips to the hole in the Swirl Pint and press "MIX-IN" button.
9. Once the program finishes, rotate the outer bowl and detach it from the machine.
10. Transfer the ice cream into serving bowls and enjoy immediately.

Per Serving: Calories: 259 | Fat: 15.2g | Sat Fat: 9.9g | Carbohydrates: 29.3g | Fiber: 0g | Sugar: 29g | Protein: 2.6g

Almond Ice Cream

Prep Time: 25 minutes | Cook Time: 1 minute | Serves: 2

Ingredients:

1 tablespoon cream cheese, softened
¾ cup heavy cream
¼ cup almonds, chopped
⅓ cup sugar, granulated
1 teaspoon almond extract
1 cup whole milk

Preparation:

1. In a large microwave-safe bowl, microwave the cream cheese for 12 seconds.
2. Remove the bowl from the microwave and add the sugar and almond extract and thoroughly whisk.
3. Slowly fold in the heavy cream and milk until completely smooth.
4. Pour the mixture into an empty Swirl Pint. Snap the lid on the pint and freeze for at least 24 hours.
5. After 24 hours, remove the pint from the freezer and take off the lid. Place the Swirl Pint in the outer bowl, then lock the outer bowl lid into place.
6. Transfer the outer bowl into the machine, twisting it into place.
7. Press the power button to turn on the unit. Select Scoop. Then select Ice Cream.
8. When the program is completed, use a spoon to create a 1½-inch (4 cm) wide hole that reaches the bottom of the processed portion of the Swirl Pint. Add the almonds to the hole in the Swirl Pint and press "MIX-IN" button.
9. Once the program finishes, rotate the outer bowl and detach it from the machine.
10. Dish out the ice cream from the pint and serve chilled.

Per Serving: Calories: 347 | Fat: 22g | Sat Fat: 7g | Carbohydrates: 27g | Fiber: 1.9g | Sugar: 21g | Protein: 11g

Zucchini and Chocolate Chip Ice Cream

Prep Time: 15 minutes | Serves: 4

Ingredients:

½ cup frozen zucchini, thawed and squeezed dry
½ cup granulated sugar
1 cup whole milk
½ teaspoon lemon extract
½ teaspoon raspberry extract
4 drops green food coloring
⅓ cup heavy cream
⅓ cup chocolate chips

Preparation:

1. In a high-powered blender, put in zucchini and remaining ingredients except for chocolate chips and process to form a smooth mixture.
2. Transfer the mixture into an empty Swirl Pint. Snap the lid on the pint and freeze for at least 24 hours.
3. After 24 hours, remove the pint from the freezer and take off the lid. Place the Swirl Pint in the outer bowl, then lock the outer bowl lid into place.
4. Transfer the outer bowl into the machine, twisting it into place.
5. Press the power button to turn on the unit. Select Scoop. Then select Ice Cream.
6. When the program is completed, use a spoon to create a 1½-inch (4 cm) wide hole that reaches the bottom of the processed portion of the Swirl Pint. Add chocolate chips to the hole in the Swirl Pint and press "MIX-IN" button.
7. Once the program finishes, rotate the outer bowl and detach it from the machine.
8. Transfer the ice cream into serving bowls and enjoy immediately.

Per Serving: Calories: 245 | Fat: 9.9g | Sat Fat: 6.4g | Carbohydrates: 37g | Fiber: 0.6g | Sugar: 35.8g | Protein: 3.4g

Peach Granola Ice Cream

Prep Time: 10 minutes | Serves: 4

Ingredients:

1 (15¼-ounce) can peaches in heavy syrup, drained and divided
12 ounces peach yogurt
1 teaspoon sugar
½ teaspoon vanilla extract
¼ teaspoon ground cinnamon
¼ cup honey granola

Preparation:

1. Place half of peaches, yogurt, sugar, vanilla extract and cinnamon in an empty Ninja Swirl pint container and blend to incorporate.
2. Snap the lid on the pint and freeze for at least 24 hours.
3. After 24 hours, remove the pint from the freezer and take off the lid. Place the Swirl Pint in the outer bowl, then lock the outer bowl lid into place.
4. Transfer the outer bowl into the machine, twisting it into place. Press the power button to turn on the unit. Select Scoop. Then select Ice Cream.
5. When the program is completed, use a spoon to create a 1½-inch (4 cm) wide hole that reaches the bottom of the processed portion of the Swirl Pint. Add remaining peaches and granola to the hole in the Swirl Pint and press "MIX-IN" button.
6. Once the program finishes, rotate the outer bowl and detach it from the machine.
7. Transfer the ice cream into serving bowls and enjoy immediately.

Per Serving: Calories: 322 | Fat: 3.4g | Sat Fat: 1.4g | Carbohydrates: 66.1g | Fiber: 9.4g | Sugar: 63g | Protein: 10.9g

Strawberry and Graham Cracker Ice Cream

Prep Time: 10 minutes | Serves: 4

Ingredients:

1 (11.5 ounce) bottle strawberry protein shake
½ cup cottage cheese
¼ teaspoon strawberry extract
½ cup fresh strawberries, cut up
½ graham cracker, broken into pieces

Preparation:

1. In a high-powered blender, put in protein shake, cottage cheese, and strawberry extract and process to form a smooth mixture.
2. Transfer the blended mixture into an empty Ninja Swirl pint container.
3. Snap the lid on the pint and freeze for at least 24 hours.
4. After 24 hours, remove the pint from the freezer and take off the lid. Place the Swirl Pint in the outer bowl, then lock the outer bowl lid into place.
5. Transfer the outer bowl into the machine, twisting it into place.
6. Press the power button to turn on the unit. Select Scoop. Then select Ice Cream.
7. When the program is completed, use a spoon to create a 1½-inch (4 cm) wide hole that reaches the bottom of the processed portion of the Swirl Pint. Add strawberries and graham cracker to the hole in the Swirl Pint and press "MIX-IN" button.
8. Once the program finishes, rotate the outer bowl and detach it from the machine.
9. Transfer the ice cream into serving bowls and enjoy immediately.
Per Serving: Calories: 83 | Fat: 1.7g | Sat Fat: 0.9g | Carbohydrates: 4.5g | Fiber: 0.4g | Sugar: 2.4g | Protein: 12.1g

Strawberry and Sugar Cookies Ice Cream

Prep Time: 15 minutes | Cook Time: 5 minutes | Serves: 4

Ingredients:

1 cup fresh strawberries, chopped
¼ cup plus 1 teaspoon sugar, divided
½ teaspoon lime juice
1 cup milk
½ cup half-and-half
2 tablespoons instant banana pudding mix
2 sugar cookies, crushed
1 teaspoon butter, melted

Preparation:

1. In a small saucepan, put in the strawberries, ¼ cup of sugar, and lime juice on burner at around medium heat.
2. Cook for about 5 minutes, stirring continuously.
3. Take off the pan of filling from burner and set aside to cool.
4. In an empty Ninja Swirl pint container, put in milk, half-and-half and banana pudding mix and with a wire whisk, whisk to incorporate thoroughly.
5. Put in filling mixture and blend to incorporate thoroughly.
6. Snap the lid on the pint and freeze for at least 24 hours.
7. After 24 hours, remove the pint from the freezer and take off the lid. Place the Swirl Pint in the outer bowl, then lock the outer bowl lid into place.
8. Transfer the outer bowl into the machine, twisting it into place.
9. Press the power button to turn on the unit. Select Scoop. Then select Ice Cream.
10. Meanwhile, in a medium-sized bowl, put in sugar cookies, butter and remaining sugar and blend to incorporate thoroughly.
11. When the program is completed, use a spoon to create a 1½-inch (4 cm) wide hole that reaches the bottom of the processed portion of the Swirl Pint. Add cookie mixture to the hole in the Swirl Pint and press "MIX-IN" button.
12. Once the program finishes, rotate the outer bowl and detach it from the machine.
13. Transfer the ice cream into serving bowls and enjoy immediately.
Per Serving: Calories: 257 | Fat: 12.1g | Sat Fat: 6.7g | Carbohydrates: 235.4g | Fiber: 0.7g | Sugar: 25.7g | Protein: 4.4g

Cinnamon Oatmeal Raisin Cookies Ice Cream

Prep Time: 10 minutes | Serves: 4

Ingredients:

1 cup milk
½ cup brown sugar
2 tablespoons cream cheese
¼ teaspoon ground cinnamon
¼ cup oatmeal raisin cookies, crumbled

Preparation:

1. In a high-powered blender, put in milk, brown sugar, cream cheese and cinnamon and process to form a smooth mixture.
2. Pour the mixture into an empty Swirl Pint. Snap the lid on the pint and freeze for at least 24 hours.
3. After 24 hours, remove the pint from the freezer and take off the lid. Place the Swirl Pint in the outer bowl, then lock the outer bowl lid into place.
4. Transfer the outer bowl into the machine, twisting it into place.
5. Press the power button to turn on the unit. Select Scoop. Then select Ice Cream.
6. When the program is completed, use a spoon to create a 1½-inch (4 cm) wide hole that reaches the bottom of the processed portion of the Swirl Pint. Add cookies to the hole in the Swirl Pint and press "MIX-IN" button.
7. Once the program finishes, rotate the outer bowl and detach it from the machine.
8. Transfer the ice cream into serving bowls and enjoy immediately.
Per Serving: Calories: 185 | Fat: 5.6g | Sat Fat: 1.9g | Carbohydrates: 31.5g | Fiber: 0.8g | Sugar: 26.4g | Protein: 3.9g

Butter Sandwich Cookies Ice Cream

Prep Time: 15 minutes | Cook Time: 10 seconds | Serves: 4

Ingredients:

1 tablespoon cream cheese
⅓ cup granulated sugar
1 teaspoon almond extract
1 cup whole milk
¾ cup heavy cream
3 butter cream sandwich cookies, broken

Preparation:

1. In a large microwave-safe bowl, put in the cream cheese and microwave on High for about 10 seconds.
2. Take off from the microwave and blend until smooth.
3. Put in sugar and almond extract and with a wire whisk, beat until the mixture looks like frosting.
4. Slowly Put in milk and heavy cream and whisk until blended thoroughly.
5. Pour the mixture into an empty Swirl Pint. Snap the lid on the pint and freeze for at least 24 hours.
6. After 24 hours, remove the pint from the freezer and take off the lid. Place the Swirl Pint in the outer bowl, then lock the outer bowl lid into place.
7. Transfer the outer bowl into the machine, twisting it into place.
8. Press the power button to turn on the unit. Select Scoop. Then select Ice Cream
9. When the program is completed, use a spoon to create a 1½-inch (4 cm) wide hole that reaches the bottom of the processed portion of the Swirl Pint. Add crushed cookies to the hole in the Swirl Pint and press "MIX-IN" button.
10. Once the program finishes, rotate the outer bowl and detach it from the machine.
11. Transfer the ice cream into serving bowls and enjoy immediately.
Per Serving: Calories: 286 | Fat: 15.7g | Sat Fat: 7.6g | Carbohydrates: 34.5g | Fiber: 0.8g | Sugar: 26g | Protein: 4.1g

Caramel Banana Chocolate Chips Ice Cream

Prep Time: 10 minutes | Serves: 4

> Ingredients:

1 (11.5 ounce) bottle caramel protein shake
1 small banana, peel removed
1 tablespoon chocolate chips, cut up

> Preparation:

1. In a high-powered blender, put in protein shake and banana and process to form a smooth mixture.
2. Transfer the mixture into an empty Swirl Pint. Snap the lid on the pint and freeze for at least 24 hours.
3. After 24 hours, remove the pint from the freezer and take off the lid. Place the Swirl Pint in the outer bowl, then lock the outer bowl lid into place.
4. Transfer the outer bowl into the machine, twisting it into place.
5. Press the power button to turn on the unit. Select Scoop. Then select Ice Cream.
6. When the program is completed, use a spoon to create a 1½-inch (4 cm) wide hole that reaches the bottom of the processed portion of the Swirl Pint. Add chocolate chips to the hole in the Swirl Pint and press "MIX-IN" button.
7. Once the program finishes, rotate the outer bowl and detach it from the machine.
8. Transfer the ice cream into serving bowls and enjoy immediately.

Per Serving: Calories: 369 | Fat: 3.9g | Sat Fat: 2.1g | Carbohydrates: 19.4g | Fiber: 0.8g | Sugar: 4.4g | Protein: 36.9g

Pecan and Raspberry Jam Ice Cream

Prep Time: 10 minutes | Cook Time: 5 minutes | Serves: 4

> Ingredients:

1 cup heavy cream
½ cup whole milk
¼ cup maple syrup
2 ounces ricotta cheese
2 tablespoons raspberry jam
2 tablespoons lime curd
¼ cup pecans, chopped

> Preparation:

1. In a small-sized saucepan, put in cream, milk, and maple syrup on burner at around medium heat and cook until heated through, stirring continuously.
2. Add in the ricotta cheese and blend to incorporate thoroughly.
3. Transfer the mixture into an empty Ninja Swirl pint container.
4. Place the container into an ice bath to cool.
5. After cooling, cover the container with the storage lid and freeze for at least 24 hours.
6. After 24 hours, take off the lid from container and arrange into the outer bowl of Ninja Swirl.
7. Transfer the outer bowl into the machine, twisting it into place.
8. Press the power button to turn on the unit. Select Scoop. Then select Ice Cream.
9. When the program is completed, use a spoon to create a 1½-inch (4 cm) wide hole that reaches the bottom of the processed portion of the Swirl Pint. Add jam, lime curd and pecans to the hole in the Swirl Pint and press "MIX-IN" button.
10. Once the program finishes, rotate the outer bowl and detach it from the machine.
11. Transfer the ice cream into serving bowls and serve with fresh raspberries if desired.

Per Serving: Calories: 356 | Fat: 39.3g | Sat Fat: 10.3g | Carbohydrates: 27.4g | Fiber: 1.7g | Sugar: 27.4g | Protein: 5.4g

Mini Pretzel Ice Cream

Prep Time: 10 minutes | Cook Time: 1 minute | Serves: 2

Ingredients:

½ tablespoon cream cheese, softened
⅓ cup cream
1 tablespoon vanilla extract
3 tablespoons sugar
½ cup whole milk
Mix-Ins:
½ tablespoon mini pretzels

Preparation:

1. In a large microwave-safe bowl, microwave the cream cheese for 12 seconds.
2. Take off from the microwave and blend until smooth. Stir in the sugar and vanilla extract.
3. Fold in the heavy cream and milk and whisk well.
4. Pour the mixture into an empty Swirl Pint. Snap the lid on the pint and freeze for at least 24 hours.
5. After 24 hours, remove the pint from the freezer and take off the lid. Place the Swirl Pint in the outer bowl, then lock the outer bowl lid into place.
6. Transfer the outer bowl into the machine, twisting it into place.
7. Press the power button to turn on the unit. Select Scoop. Then select Ice Cream.
8. When the program is completed, use a spoon to create a 1½-inch (4 cm) wide hole that reaches the bottom of the processed portion of the Swirl Pint. Add the mini pretzels to the hole in the Swirl Pint and press "MIX-IN" button.
9. Once the program finishes, rotate the outer bowl and detach it from the machine.
10. Dish out the ice cream from the pint and serve chilled.
Per Serving: Calories: 189 | Fat: 11g | Sat Fat: 6.9g | Carbohydrates: 20g | Fiber: 0g | Sugar: 20g | Protein: 2.7g

Butterscotch and Caramel Corn Ice cream

Prep Time: 10 minutes | Serves: 6

Ingredients:

½ cup butterscotch pieces, chopped
1 cup whole milk
⅓ cup sugar, granulated
¾ cup caramel corn, roughly chopped
¾ cup heavy cream

Preparation:

1. In a blender, blitz milk with the remaining ingredients except for butterscotch pieces.
2. Pour the mixture into an empty Swirl Pint. Snap the lid on the pint and freeze for at least 24 hours.
3. After 24 hours, remove the pint from the freezer and take off the lid. Place the Swirl Pint in the outer bowl, then lock the outer bowl lid into place.
4. Transfer the outer bowl into the machine, twisting it into place.
5. Press the power button to turn on the unit. Select Scoop. Then select Ice Cream.
6. When the program is completed, use a spoon to create a 1½-inch (4 cm) wide hole that reaches the bottom of the processed portion of the Swirl Pint. Add the butterscotch pieces to the hole in the Swirl Pint and press "MIX-IN" button.
7. Once the program finishes, rotate the outer bowl and detach it from the machine.
8. Dish out the ice cream from the pint and serve chilled.
Per Serving: Calories: 185 | Fat: 10.2g | Sat Fat: 6.7g | Carbohydrates: 21g | Fiber: 0g | Sugar: 20.8g | Protein: 2.5g

Caramel Chocolate Chip Ice Cream

Prep Time: 10 minutes | Serves: 4

Ingredients:

1 (11.5 ounce) bottle caramel protein shake
2 tablespoons instant white chocolate pudding mix
2 tablespoons instant espresso powder
1 tablespoon salted caramel chocolate chips, cut up

Preparation:

1. In a high-powered blender, put in protein shake, pudding mix, and espresso powder and process to form a smooth mixture.
2. Pour the mixture into an empty Swirl Pint. Snap the lid on the pint and freeze for at least 24 hours.
3. After 24 hours, remove the pint from the freezer and take off the lid. Place the Swirl Pint in the outer bowl, then lock the outer bowl lid into place.
4. Transfer the outer bowl into the machine, twisting it into place.
5. Press the power button to turn on the unit. Select Scoop. Then select Ice Cream.
6. When the program is completed, use a spoon to create a 1½-inch (4 cm) wide hole that reaches the bottom of the processed portion of the Swirl Pint. Add chocolate chips to the hole in the Swirl Pint and press "MIX-IN" button.
7. Once the program finishes, rotate the outer bowl and detach it from the machine.
8. Transfer the ice cream into serving bowls and enjoy immediately.
Per Serving: Calories: 369 | Fat: 4.1g | Sat Fat: 1.1g | Carbohydrates: 50.6g | Fiber: 0.3g | Sugar: 37.3g | Protein: 34.4g

Lavender and Chocolate Wafer Ice Cream

Prep Time: 15 minutes | Cook Time: 10 minutes | Serves: 4

Ingredients:

¾ cup heavy cream
⅛ teaspoon salt
¾ cup whole milk
4 drops purple food coloring
1 tablespoon dried culinary lavender
½ cup condensed milk, sweetened
⅓ cup chocolate wafer cookies, crushed

Preparation:

1. In a saucepan, merge together heavy cream, lavender, and salt.
2. Cook for about 10 minutes, stirring constantly.
3. Eliminate from the heat and strain the cream mixture in a large bowl.
4. Eliminate the lavender leaves and fold in the milk, condensed milk and purple food coloring.
5. Pour the mixture into an empty Swirl Pint. Snap the lid on the pint and freeze for at least 24 hours.
6. After 24 hours, remove the pint from the freezer and take off the lid. Place the Swirl Pint in the outer bowl, then lock the outer bowl lid into place.
7. Transfer the outer bowl into the machine, twisting it into place.
8. Press the power button to turn on the unit. Select Scoop. Then select Ice Cream.
9. When the program is completed, use a spoon to create a 1½-inch (4 cm) wide hole that reaches the bottom of the processed portion of the Swirl Pint. Add crushed cookies to the hole in the Swirl Pint and press "MIX-IN" button.
10. Once the program finishes, rotate the outer bowl and detach it from the machine.
11. Dish out the ice cream from the pint and serve chilled.
Per Serving: Calories: 229 | Fat: 13.2g | Sat Fat: 8.1g | Carbohydrates: 23.5g | Fiber: 0g | Sugar: 23.2g | Protein: 5g

Kale, Cocoa and Peppermint Candy Ice Cream

Prep Time: 5 minutes | Serves: 4

Ingredients:

½ cup frozen kale, thawed, squeezed dry
1 cup whole milk
3 tablespoons dark cocoa powder
8 striped peppermint candies, roughly chopped
½ cup dark brown sugar
1 teaspoon peppermint extract
⅓ cup heavy cream

Preparation:

1. In a blender, blitz kale, brown sugar, milk, peppermint extract, and cocoa powder.
2. Pour the mixture into an empty Swirl Pint. Snap the lid on the pint and freeze for at least 24 hours.
3. After 24 hours, remove the pint from the freezer and take off the lid. Place the Swirl Pint in the outer bowl, then lock the outer bowl lid into place.
4. Transfer the outer bowl into the machine, twisting it into place.
5. Press the power button to turn on the unit. Select Scoop. Then select Ice Cream.
6. When the program is completed, use a spoon to create a 1½-inch (4 cm) wide hole that reaches the bottom of the processed portion of the Swirl Pint. Add the chopped peppermint candy pieces to the hole in the Swirl Pint and press "MIX-IN" button.
7. Once the program finishes, rotate the outer bowl and detach it from the machine.
8. Dish out the ice cream from the pint and serve chilled.

Per Serving: Calories: 148 | Fat: 5g | Sat Fat: 3g | Carbohydrates: 22g | Fiber: 0.3g | Sugar: 20g | Protein: 2g

Double Chocolate Ice Cream

Prep Time: 14 minutes | Serves: 4

Ingredients:

1 tablespoon cream cheese, softened
⅓ cup granulated sugar
2 tablespoons unsweetened cocoa powder
1 teaspoon almond extract
1 cup whole milk
¾ cup heavy cream
4 tablespoons mini chocolate chips

Preparation:

1. In a large microwave-safe bowl, put in the cream cheese and microwave on High for about 10 seconds.
2. Take off from the microwave and blend until smooth.
3. Put in sugar, cocoa powder and almond extract and with a wire whisk, beat until the mixture looks like frosting.
4. Slowly Put in milk and heavy cream and whisk to incorporate thoroughly.
5. Pour the mixture into an empty Swirl Pint. Snap the lid on the pint and freeze for at least 24 hours.
6. After 24 hours, remove the pint from the freezer and take off the lid. Place the Swirl Pint in the outer bowl, then lock the outer bowl lid into place.
7. Transfer the outer bowl into the machine, twisting it into place.
8. Press the power button to turn on the unit. Select Scoop. Then select Ice Cream.
9. When the program is completed, use a spoon to create a 1½-inch (4 cm) wide hole that reaches the bottom of the processed portion of the Swirl Pint. Add chocolate chips to the hole in the Swirl Pint and press "MIX-IN" button.
10. Once the program finishes, rotate the outer bowl and detach it from the machine.
11. Transfer the ice cream into serving bowls and enjoy immediately.

Per Serving: Calories: 251 | Fat: 14.7g | Sat Fat: 9.3g | Carbohydrates: 28g | Fiber: 1.3g | Sugar: 25.5g | Protein: 3.9g

Sea Salt Chocolate Ice Cream

Prep Time: 15 minutes | Cook Time: 7 minutes | Serves: 4

Ingredients:

2 cups whole milk
½ cup sugar
1 teaspoon vanilla extract
Pinch of sea salt
1 ounce chocolate chips
2 teaspoons butter

Preparation:

1. In a medium saucepan, put in milk and sugar and whisk to incorporate.
2. Place saucepan on burner at around medium heat and cook for around 3-5 minutes, stirring continuously.
3. Take off the pan of milk mixture from burner and whisk in vanilla extract and salt.
4. Transfer the blended mixture into an empty Ninja Swirl pint container.
5. Place the container into an ice bath to cool.
6. After cooling, snap the lid on the pint and freeze for 24 hours.
7. Meanwhile, in a medium-sized microwave-safe bowl, put in chocolate chips and butter and microwave on high for around 2 minutes, stirring after every 20 seconds.
8. Take off the bowl from microwave and blend until smooth.
9. Let the chocolate mixture to cool thoroughly.
10. After 24 hours, remove the pint from the freezer and take off the lid. Place the Swirl Pint in the outer bowl, then lock the outer bowl lid into place.
11. Transfer the outer bowl into the machine, twisting it into place.
12. Press the power button to turn on the unit. Select Scoop. Then select Ice Cream.
13. When the program is completed, use a spoon to create a 1½-inch (4 cm) wide hole that reaches the bottom of the processed portion of the Swirl Pint. Add chocolate mixture to the hole in the Swirl Pint and press "MIX-IN" button.
14. Once the program finishes, rotate the outer bowl and detach it from the machine.
15. Transfer the ice cream into serving bowls and enjoy immediately.

Per Serving: Calories: 225 | Fat: 8g | Sat Fat: 5g | Carbohydrates: 34.9g | Fiber: 0.2g | Sugar: 35.2g | Protein: 4.5g

Chapter 5 Gelato

Pistachio Gelato

Ingredients:

4 large egg yolks
5 tablespoons granulated sugar
1 tablespoon honey
1 cup heavy cream
⅓ cup whole milk
1 teaspoon vanilla extract
⅓ cup pistachios, chopped

Preparation:

1. In a small saucepan, put in the egg yolks, sugar and honey and whisk until blended thoroughly.
2. Put in heavy cream, milk and vanilla extract and whisk until blended thoroughly.
3. Place the saucepan on burner at around medium heat and cook for 2-3 minutes, stirring continuously.
4. Take off the saucepan of milk mixture from burner and through a fine-mesh strainer, strain the blended mixture into an empty Ninja Swirl pint container.
5. Place the container into an ice bath to cool.
6. After cooling, snap the lid on the pint and freeze for at least 24 hours.
7. After 24 hours, remove the pint from the freezer and take off the lid. Place the Swirl Pint in the outer bowl, then lock the outer bowl lid into place.
8. Transfer the outer bowl into the machine, twisting it into place.
9. Press the power button to turn on the unit. Select Scoop. Then select Gelato.
10. When the program is completed, use a spoon to create a 1½-inch (4 cm) wide hole that reaches the bottom of the processed portion of the Swirl Pint. Add pistachios to the hole in the Swirl Pint and press "MIX-IN" button.
11. Once the program finishes, rotate the outer bowl and detach it from the machine.
12. Transfer the gelato into serving bowls and enjoy immediately.

Per Serving: Calories: 271 | Fat: 18.6g | Sat Fat: 9.2g | Carbohydrates: 23.2g | Fiber: 0.5g | Sugar: 21g | Protein: 5g

Homemade Sugar Cookie Gelato

Ingredients:

1 cup whole milk
¾ cup heavy cream
⅓ cup granulated sugar
¼ cup sugar cookie mix
2 egg yolks
1 teaspoon vanilla extract

Preparation:

1. In a medium saucepan, add milk and remaining ingredients on burner at around medium heat and cook for around 5 minutes, whisking constantly.
2. Through a fine-mesh strainer, strain the mixture into an empty Ninja Swirl pint container.
3. Place the container into an ice bath to cool.
4. After cooling, snap the lid on the pint and freeze for at least 24 hours.
5. After 24 hours, remove the pint from the freezer and take off the lid. Place the Swirl Pint in the outer bowl, then lock the outer bowl lid into place.
6. Transfer the outer bowl into the machine, twisting it into place.
7. Press the power button to turn on the unit. Select Scoop. Then select Gelato.
8. Once the program finishes, rotate the outer bowl and detach it from the machine.
9. Transfer the gelato into serving bowls and serve immediately.

Per Serving: Calories: 263 | Fat: 13.8g | Sat Fat: 7.4g | Carbohydrates: 31.2g | Fiber: 0g | Sugar: 26.2g | Protein: 4.3g

Blueberry Gelato

Prep Time: 15 minutes | Cook Time: 10 minutes | Serves: 4

Ingredients:

1 cup whole milk
½ cup heavy cream
3 large egg yolks
⅓ cup granulated sugar
1 tablespoon honey
½ cup fresh blueberries

Preparation:

1. In a medium-sized saucepan, add milk and remaining ingredients except for blueberries pieces on burner at around medium heat.
2. Cook for around 7-10 minutes, whisking constantly.
3. Through a fine-mesh strainer, strain the blended mixture into an empty Ninja Swirl pint container.
4. Place the container into an ice bath to cool.
5. After cooling, blend in the blueberries pieces.
6. Snap the lid on the pint and freeze for at least 24 hours.
7. After 24 hours, remove the pint from the freezer and take off the lid. Place the Swirl Pint in the outer bowl, then lock the outer bowl lid into place.
8. Transfer the outer bowl into the machine, twisting it into place.
9. Press the power button to turn on the unit. Select Scoop. Then select Gelato.
10. Once the program finishes, rotate the outer bowl and detach it from the machine.
11. Transfer the gelato into serving bowls and enjoy immediately.
Per Serving: Calories: 219 | Fat: 11.2g | Sat Fat: 6g | Carbohydrates: 27.1g | Fiber: 1.4g | Sugar: 24.9g | Protein: 4.6g

Strawberry Shortbread Cookies Gelato

Prep Time: 10 minutes | Cook Time: 3 minutes | Serves: 4

Ingredients:

4 large egg yolks
3 tablespoons granulated sugar
3 tablespoons strawberry preserves
1 teaspoon vanilla extract
1 cup whole milk
⅓ cup heavy cream
¼ cup cream cheese, softened
3 large shortbread cookies, broken in 1-inch pieces

Preparation:

1. In a small saucepan, put in the egg yolks, sugar, strawberry preserves and vanilla extract and whisk until blended thoroughly.
2. Put in milk, heavy cream and cream cheese and whisk until blended thoroughly.
3. Place the saucepan on burner at around medium heat and cook for 2 to 3 minutes, stirring continuously.
4. Take off the saucepan of milk mixture from burner and through a fine-mesh strainer, strain the blended mixture into an empty Ninja Swirl pint container.
5. Place the container into an ice bath to cool.
6. After cooling, snap the lid on the pint and freeze for at least 24 hours.
7. After 24 hours, remove the pint from the freezer and take off the lid. Place the Swirl Pint in the outer bowl, then lock the outer bowl lid into place.
8. Transfer the outer bowl into the machine, twisting it into place.
9. Press the power button to turn on the unit. Select Scoop. Then select Gelato.
10. When the program is completed, use a spoon to create a 1½-inch (4 cm) wide hole that reaches the bottom of the processed portion of the Swirl Pint. Add cookies to the hole in the Swirl Pint and press "MIX-IN" button.
11. Once the program finishes, rotate the outer bowl and detach it from the machine.
12. Transfer the gelato into serving bowls and enjoy immediately.
Per Serving: Calories: 281 | Fat: 16.6g | Sat Fat: 9g | Carbohydrates: 27.1g | Fiber: 0.2g | Sugar: 21.6g | Protein: 6.3g

Chocolate Gelato

Prep Time: 10 minutes | Cook Time: 5 minutes | Serves: 4

Ingredients:

1 cup whole milk
¾ cup heavy cream
⅓ cup granulated sugar
⅓ cup dark chocolate chunks
2 egg yolks
2 tablespoons unsweetened cocoa powder
1 teaspoon vanilla extract

Preparation:

1. In a medium saucepan, combine the milk and remaining ingredients on burner at around medium heat and cook for around 5 minutes, whisking constantly.
2. Through a fine-mesh strainer, strain the mixture into an empty Ninja Swirl pint container.
3. Place the container into an ice bath to cool.
4. After cooling, snap the lid on the pint and freeze for at least 24 hours.
5. After 24 hours, remove the pint from the freezer and take off the lid. Place the Swirl Pint in the outer bowl, then lock the outer bowl lid into place.
6. Transfer the outer bowl into the machine, twisting it into place.
7. Press the power button to turn on the unit. Select Scoop. Then select Gelato.
8. Once the program finishes, rotate the outer bowl and detach it from the machine.
9. Transfer the gelato into serving bowls and serve immediately.
Per Serving: Calories: 288 | Fat: 17.1g | Sat Fat: 10.3g | Carbohydrates: 30.3g | Fiber: 1.4g | Sugar: 27.3g | Protein: 5.4g

Sweet Potato and Graham Cracker Gelato

Prep Time: 10 minutes | Cook Time: 3 minutes | Serves: 4

Ingredients:

4 large egg yolks
1 cup heavy cream
⅓ cup granulated sugar
½ of banana, peeled and sliced
½ cup frozen sweet potato, chopped
1 (3½-ounce) box cheesecake pudding mix
4 graham crackers, crumbled

Preparation:

1. In a small saucepan, put in the egg yolks, heavy cream and sugar and whisk until blended thoroughly.
2. Place the saucepan on burner at around medium heat and cook for 2 to 3 minutes, stirring continuously.
3. Take off the saucepan of egg mixture from burner and through a fine-mesh strainer, strain the blended mixture into an empty Ninja Swirl pint container.
4. Place the container into an ice bath to cool.
5. After cooling, put in in the banana, sweet potato and pudding until blended thoroughly.
6. Snap the lid on the pint and freeze for at least 24 hours.
7. After 24 hours, remove the pint from the freezer and take off the lid. Place the Swirl Pint in the outer bowl, then lock the outer bowl lid into place.
8. Transfer the outer bowl into the machine, twisting it into place.
9. Press the power button to turn on the unit. Select Scoop. Then select Gelato.
10. When the program is completed, use a spoon to create a 1½-inch (4 cm) wide hole that reaches the bottom of the processed portion of the Swirl Pint. Add crackers to the hole in the Swirl Pint and press "MIX-IN" button.
11. Once the program finishes, rotate the outer bowl and detach it from the machine.
12. Transfer the gelato into serving bowls and enjoy immediately.
Per Serving: Calories: 404 | Fat: 17.1g | Sat Fat: 8.8g | Carbohydrates: 59.3g | Fiber: 2.6g | Sugar: 24.6g | Protein: 5g

Mango Gelato

Prep Time: 15 minutes | Cook Time: 3 minutes | Serves: 4

Ingredients:

3 large egg yolks
½ cup plus 2 tablespoons granulated sugar, divided
1 tablespoon honey
½ cup crème fraîche
¾ cup whole milk
¼ cup heavy cream
½ teaspoon vanilla extract
1 cup frozen mango chunks

Preparation:

1. In a small saucepan, put in the egg yolks, ½ cup of sugar and honey and whisk until blended thoroughly.
2. Put in crème fraîche, milk, heavy cream and vanilla extract and whisk until blended thoroughly.
3. Place the saucepan on burner at around medium heat and cook for 2 to 3 minutes, stirring continuously.
4. Take off the saucepan of milk mixture from burner and through a fine-mesh strainer, strain the blended mixture into an empty Ninja Swirl pint container.
5. Place the container into an ice bath to cool.
6. After cooling, Snap the lid on the pint and freeze for at least 24 hours.
7. Meanwhile, in a small-sized saucepan, put in the mango chunks and remaining sugar on burner at around medium heat and cook for about 8 minutes, stirring occasionally and mashing to form a thick jam.
8. Take off the saucepan of mango mixture from burner and transfer the jam into a bowl.
9. Refrigerate the jam until using.
10. After 24 hours, remove the pint from the freezer and take off the lid. Place the Swirl Pint in the outer bowl, then lock the outer bowl lid into place.
11. Transfer the outer bowl into the machine, twisting it into place.
12. Press the power button to turn on the unit. Select Scoop. Then select Gelato.
13. When the program is completed, use a spoon to create a 1½-inch (4 cm) wide hole that reaches the bottom of the processed portion of the Swirl Pint. Add mango jam to the hole in the Swirl Pint and press "MIX-IN" button.
14. Once the program finishes, rotate the outer bowl and detach it from the machine.
15. Transfer the gelato into serving bowls and enjoy immediately.

Per Serving: Calories: 249 | Fat: 9.5g | Sat Fat: 4.9g | Carbohydrates: 39.3g | Fiber: 0.7g | Sugar: 38.1g | Protein: 4.2g

Raspberry Gelato

Prep Time: 15 minutes | Cook Time: 10 minutes | Serves: 4

Ingredients:

1 cup whole milk
½ cup heavy cream
3 large egg yolks
⅓ cup granulated sugar
1 tablespoon honey
½ cup fresh raspberries, roughly chopped

Preparation:

1. In a medium saucepan, put in milk and remaining ingredients except for raspberry pieces on burner at around medium heat.
2. Cook for around 7-10 minutes, whisking constantly.
3. Through a fine-mesh strainer, strain the blended mixture into an empty Ninja Swirl pint container.
4. Place the container into an ice bath to cool.
5. After cooling, blend in the raspberry pieces.
6. Snap the lid on the pint and freeze for at least 24 hours.
7. After 24 hours, remove the pint from the freezer and take off the lid. Place the Swirl Pint in the outer bowl, then lock the outer bowl lid into place.
8. Transfer the outer bowl into the machine, twisting it into place.
9. Press the power button to turn on the unit. Select Scoop. Then select Gelato. Let the cycle complete.
10. Lift the Swirl Pint out of the outer bowl.
11. Transfer the gelato into serving bowls and enjoy immediately.

Per Serving: Calories: 215 | Fat: 11g | Sat Fat: 5.8g | Carbohydrates: 26.5g | Fiber: 1g | Sugar: 25g | Protein: 4.5g

Peanut Gelato

Prep Time: 15 minutes | Cook Time: 9 minutes | Serves: 4

Ingredients:

1½ cups full-fat coconut milk
⅓ cup sugar
1 tablespoon cornstarch
3 tablespoons peanut butter
3 dark chocolate peanut butter cups, cut up
2 tablespoons peanuts, cut up

Preparation:

1. In a small saucepan, combine the coconut milk, sugar, and cornstarch on burner at around medium heat and whisk to incorporate.
2. Cook the mixture until boiling.
3. Immediately turn down the heat to low and cook for around 3-4 minutes.
4. Take off the pan of sugar mixture from burner and whisk in the peanut butter.
5. Transfer the mixture into an empty Ninja Swirl pint container.
6. Place the container into an ice bath to cool.
7. After cooling, snap the lid on the pint and freeze for at least 24 hours.
8. After 24 hours, remove the pint from the freezer and take off the lid. Place the Swirl Pint in the outer bowl, then lock the outer bowl lid into place.
9. Transfer the outer bowl into the machine, twisting it into place.
10. Press the power button to turn on the unit. Select Scoop. Then select Gelato.
11. When the program is completed, with a spoon, create a 1½-inch wide hole in the center that reaches the bottom of the Swirl pint container.
12. Add the peanut butter cups and peanuts into the hole and press "MIX-IN" button.
13. Once the program finishes, rotate the outer bowl and detach it from the machine.
14. Transfer the gelato into serving bowls and serve immediately.

Per Serving: Calories: 450 | Fat: 34g | Sat Fat: 23.2g | Carbohydrates: 31.3g | Fiber: 1.1g | Sugar: 24.6g | Protein: 7.2g

Apricot and Pistachio Gelato

Prep Time: 10 minutes | Cook Time: 3 minutes | Serves: 4

Ingredients:

4 large egg yolks
3 tablespoons granulated sugar
3 tablespoons apricot jam
1 teaspoon vanilla extract
1 cup whole milk
⅓ cup heavy cream
¼ cup mascarpone cheese, softened
¼ cup pistachios, chopped

Preparation:

1. In a small saucepan, add egg yolks, sugar, apricot jam and vanilla extract and whisk to incorporate thoroughly.
2. Add the milk, heavy cream and mascarpone cheese and whisk to incorporate thoroughly.
3. Place the saucepan on burner at around medium heat and cook for around 2-3 minutes, stirring continuously.
4. Take off the saucepan of milk mixture from burner and through a fine-mesh strainer, strain the mixture into an empty Ninja Swirl pint container.
5. Place the container into an ice bath to cool.
6. After cooling, snap the lid on the pint and freeze for at least 24 hours.
7. After 24 hours, remove the pint from the freezer and take off the lid. Place the Swirl Pint in the outer bowl, then lock the outer bowl lid into place.
8. Transfer the outer bowl into the machine, twisting it into place.
9. Press the power button to turn on the unit. Select Scoop. Then select Gelato.
10. When the program is completed, with a spoon, create a 1½-inch wide hole in the center that reaches the bottom of the Swirl pint container.
11. Add the pistachios into the hole and press "MIX-IN" button.
12. Once the program finishes, rotate the outer bowl and detach it from the machine.
13. Transfer the gelato into serving bowls and serve immediately.

Per Serving: Calories: 269 | Fat: 15g | Sat Fat: 1.8g | Carbohydrates: 27.3g | Fiber: 0.1g | Sugar: 22.7g | Protein: 5.4g

Vanilla Gelato

Prep Time: 10 minutes | Cook Time: 5 minutes | Serves: 4

> Ingredients:

1 cup whole milk
¾ cup heavy cream
2 egg yolks
⅓ cup granulated sugar
1 teaspoon vanilla bean paste

> Preparation:

1. In a medium saucepan, combine the milk and remaining ingredients on burner at around medium heat and cook for around 5 minutes, whisking constantly.
2. Through a fine-mesh strainer, strain the mixture into an empty Ninja Swirl pint container.
3. Place the container into an ice bath to cool.
4. After cooling, snap the lid on the pint and freeze for at least 24 hours.
5. After 24 hours, remove the pint from the freezer and take off the lid. Place the Swirl Pint in the outer bowl, then lock the outer bowl lid into place.
6. Transfer the outer bowl into the machine, twisting it into place.
7. Press the power button to turn on the unit. Select Scoop. Then select Gelato.
8. Once the program finishes, rotate the outer bowl and detach it from the machine.
9. Transfer the gelato into serving bowls and serve immediately.
Per Serving: Calories: 209 | Fat: 12.6g | Sat Fat: 7.1g | Carbohydrates: 21.6g | Fiber: 0g | Sugar: 21.2g | Protein: 3.8g

Spiced Pumpkin Gelato

Prep Time: 15 minutes | Cook Time: 3 minutes | Serves: 4

> Ingredients:

3 large egg yolks
⅓ cup coconut sugar
1 tablespoon corn syrup
½ cup heavy cream
1 cup whole milk
½ cup pumpkin puree
½ teaspoon ground cinnamon
½ teaspoon ground nutmeg
¾ teaspoon vanilla extract

> Preparation:

1. In a small saucepan, put in the egg yolks, coconut sugar and corn syrup and whisk until blended thoroughly.
2. Put in heavy cream, whole milk, pumpkin puree and spices and whisk until blended thoroughly.
3. Place the saucepan on burner at around medium heat and cook for 2 to 3 minutes, stirring continuously.
4. Take off the pan of milk mixture from burner and blend in the vanilla extract.
5. Through a fine-mesh strainer, strain the blended mixture into an empty Ninja Swirl pint container.
6. Place the container into an ice bath to cool.
7. After cooling, snap the lid on the pint and freeze for at least 24 hours.
8. After 24 hours, remove the pint from the freezer and take off the lid. Place the Swirl Pint in the outer bowl, then lock the outer bowl lid into place.
9. Transfer the outer bowl into the machine, twisting it into place.
10. Press the power button to turn on the unit. Select Scoop. Then select Gelato. Let the cycle complete.
11. Transfer the gelato into serving bowls and enjoy immediately.
Per Serving: Calories: 217 | Fat: 11.1g | Sat Fat: 5.9g | Carbohydrates: 26.2g | Fiber: 1.1g | Sugar: 21.8g | Protein: 4.7g

Vanilla Brownie Gelato

Prep Time: 10 minutes | Cook Time: 5 minutes | Serves: 4

Ingredients:

1 cup whole milk
¾ cup heavy cream
⅓ cup granulated sugar
¼ cup brownie mix
2 egg yolks
1 teaspoon vanilla extract
Pinch of salt

Preparation:

1. In a medium saucepan, put in milk and remaining ingredients on burner at around medium heat and cook for around 5 minutes, whisking constantly.
2. Through a fine-mesh strainer, strain the mixture into an empty Ninja Swirl pint container.
3. Place the container into an ice bath to cool.
4. After cooling, snap the lid on the pint and freeze for at least 24 hours.
5. After 24 hours, remove the pint from the freezer and take off the lid. Place the Swirl Pint in the outer bowl, then lock the outer bowl lid into place.
6. Transfer the outer bowl into the machine, twisting it into place.
7. Press the power button to turn on the unit. Select Scoop. Then select Gelato.
8. Once the program finishes, rotate the outer bowl and detach it from the machine.
9. Transfer the gelato into serving bowls and serve immediately.
Per Serving: Calories: 266 | Fat: 14.6g | Sat Fat: 7.5g | Carbohydrates: 31g | Fiber: 0g | Sugar: 20.1g | Protein: 4.3g

Hazelnut Gelato

Prep Time: 10 minutes | Cook Time: 3 minutes | Serves: 4

Ingredients:

4 large egg yolks
5 tablespoons granulated sugar
1 tablespoon honey
1 cup heavy cream
⅓ cup whole milk
½ teaspoon vanilla extract
⅓ cup hazelnuts, chopped

Preparation:

1. In a small saucepan, add the egg yolks, sugar and honey and whisk to incorporate thoroughly.
2. Put in heavy cream, milk and vanilla extract and whisk to incorporate thoroughly.
3. Place the saucepan on burner at around medium heat and cook for around 2-3 minutes, stirring continuously.
4. Take off the saucepan of milk mixture from burner and through a fine-mesh strainer, strain the blended mixture into an empty Ninja Swirl pint container.
5. Place the container into an ice bath to cool.
6. After cooling, snap the lid on the pint and freeze for at least 24 hours.
7. After 24 hours, remove the pint from the freezer and take off the lid. Place the Swirl Pint in the outer bowl, then lock the outer bowl lid into place.
8. Transfer the outer bowl into the machine, twisting it into place.
9. Press the power button to turn on the unit. Select Scoop. Then select Gelato.
10. When the program is completed, with a spoon, create a 1½-inch wide hole in the center that reaches the bottom of the Swirl pint container.
11. Put in hazelnuts into the hole and press "MIX-IN" button.
12. Once the program finishes, rotate the outer bowl and detach it from the machine.
13. Transfer the gelato into serving bowls and enjoy immediately.
Per Serving: Calories: 269 | Fat: 18g | Sat Fat: 8.1g | Carbohydrates: 22.7g | Fiber: 0.1g | Sugar: 19.2g | Protein: 4.9g

Strawberry Gelato

Prep Time: 15 minutes | Cook Time: 10 minutes | Serves: 4

Ingredients:

1 cup whole milk
½ cup heavy cream
3 large egg yolks
⅓ cup granulated sugar
1 tablespoon corn syrup
½ cup fresh strawberries, quartered

Preparation:

1. In a medium-sized saucepan, add milk and remaining ingredients except for strawberries on burner at around medium heat and cook for around 7-10 minutes, whisking constantly.
2. Through a fine-mesh strainer, strain the mixture into an empty Ninja Swirl pint container.
3. Place the container into an ice bath to cool.
4. After cooling, stir in the strawberry pieces.
5. Snap the lid on the pint and freeze for at least 24 hours.
6. After 24 hours, remove the pint from the freezer and take off the lid. Place the Swirl Pint in the outer bowl, then lock the outer bowl lid into place.
7. Transfer the outer bowl into the machine, twisting it into place.
8. Press the power button to turn on the unit. Select Scoop. Then select Gelato.
9. Once the program finishes, rotate the outer bowl and detach it from the machine.
10. Transfer the gelato into serving bowls and serve immediately.

Per Serving: Calories: 210 | Fat: 11g | Sat Fat: 5.8g | Carbohydrates: 25.3g | Fiber: 0.4g | Sugar: 22.1g | Protein: 4.4g

Delicious Peach Gelato

Prep Time: 10 minutes | Cook Time: 8 minutes | Serves: 4

Ingredients:

3 large egg yolks
½ cup plus 2 tablespoons granulated sugar, divided
1 tablespoon maple syrup
½ cup cream cheese
¾ cup whole milk
¼ cup heavy cream
½ teaspoon vanilla extract
1 cup frozen peach chunks

Preparation:

1. In a small saucepan, add the egg yolks, ½ cup of sugar and maple syrup and whisk to incorporate thoroughly.
2. Put in cream cheese, milk, heavy cream and vanilla extract and whisk to incorporate thoroughly.
3. Place the saucepan on burner at around medium heat and cook for around 2-3 minutes, stirring continuously.
4. Take off the saucepan of milk mixture from burner and through a fine-mesh strainer, strain the blended mixture into an empty Ninja Swirl pint container.
5. Place the container into an ice bath to cool.
6. After cooling, snap the lid on the pint and freeze for at least 24 hours.
7. Meanwhile, in a small-sized saucepan, put in the peach chunks and remaining sugar on burner at around medium heat.
8. Cook for around 8 minutes, stirring occasionally and mashing to form a thick jam.
9. Take off the saucepan of berry mixture from burner and transfer the jam into a bowl.
10. Refrigerate the jam until using.
11. After 24 hours, remove the pint from the freezer and take off the lid. Place the Swirl Pint in the outer bowl, then lock the outer bowl lid into place.
12. Transfer the outer bowl into the machine, twisting it into place.
13. Press the power button to turn on the unit. Select Scoop. Then select Gelato.
14. When the program is completed, with a spoon, create a 1½-inch wide hole in the center that reaches the bottom of the Swirl pint container.
15. Put in peach jam into the hole and press "MIX-IN" button.
16. Once the program finishes, rotate the outer bowl and detach it from the machine.
17. Transfer the gelato into serving bowls and enjoy immediately.

Per Serving: Calories: 260 | Fat: 9.7g | Sat Fat: 4.9g | Carbohydrates: 42.3g | Fiber: 2.7g | Sugar: 40.4g | Protein: 4.3g

Snickerdoodle Cookie Gelato

Prep Time: 10 minutes | Cook Time: 5 minutes | Serves: 4

Ingredients:

1 cup whole milk
¾ cup heavy cream
⅓ cup granulated sugar
¼ cup snickerdoodle cookie mix
2 egg yolks
1 teaspoon vanilla extract

Preparation:

1. In a medium saucepan, add milk and remaining ingredients on burner at around medium heat and cook for around 5 minutes, whisking constantly.
2. Through a fine-mesh strainer, strain the mixture into an empty Ninja Swirl pint container.
3. Place the container into an ice bath to cool.
4. After cooling, snap the lid on the pint and freeze for at least 24 hours.
5. After 24 hours, remove the pint from the freezer and take off the lid. Place the Swirl Pint in the outer bowl, then lock the outer bowl lid into place.
6. Transfer the outer bowl into the machine, twisting it into place.
7. Press the power button to turn on the unit. Select Scoop. Then select Gelato.
8. Once the program finishes, rotate the outer bowl and detach it from the machine.
9. Transfer the gelato into serving bowls and serve immediately.

Per Serving: Calories: 250 | Fat: 12.6g | Sat Fat: 7.1g | Carbohydrates: 27.9g | Fiber: 1.4g | Sugar: 20.1g | Protein: 7.6g

Cacao Gelato

Prep Time: 10 minutes | Cook Time: 3 minutes | Serves: 4

Ingredients:

4 large egg yolks
¼ cup granulated sugar
2 tablespoons cacao powder
1 cup whole milk
⅓ cup heavy whipping cream
¼ cup cream cheese, softened
1 teaspoon vanilla extract

Preparation:

1. In a small saucepan, add the egg yolks, sugar and cacao powder and whisk until blended thoroughly.
2. Put in milk, heavy cream, cream cheese and vanilla extract and whisk until blended thoroughly.
3. Place the saucepan on burner at around medium heat and cook for 2 to 3 minutes, stirring continuously.
4. Take off the saucepan of milk mixture from burner and through a fine-mesh strainer, strain the blended mixture into an empty Ninja Swirl pint container.
5. Place the container into an ice bath to cool.
6. After cooling, snap the lid on the pint and freeze for at least 24 hours.
7. After 24 hours, remove the pint from the freezer and take off the lid. Place the Swirl Pint in the outer bowl, then lock the outer bowl lid into place.
8. Transfer the outer bowl into the machine, twisting it into place.
9. Press the power button to turn on the unit. Select Scoop. Then select Gelato.
10. Once the program finishes, rotate the outer bowl and detach it from the machine.
11. Transfer the gelato into serving bowls and enjoy immediately.

Per Serving: Calories: 232 | Fat: 15.8g | Sat Fat: 8.6g | Carbohydrates: 17.9g | Fiber: 0.8g | Sugar: 16g | Protein: 6.5g

Caramel Hazelnut Gelato

Prep Time: 10 minutes | Cook Time: 10 minutes | Serves: 4

Ingredients:

¼ cup honey
¾ cup whole milk
½ cup hazelnut creamer
2 eggs
3 tablespoons granulated sugar
¼ cup caramels, chopped

Preparation:

1. In a medium saucepan, put in honey on burner at around medium-high heat and cook for around 2-3 minutes.
2. Take off the saucepan from burner and slowly whisk in the milk and creamer.
3. Return the pan on burner at around medium-high heat and whisk in the eggs and sugar.
4. Cook for around 4-5 minutes, stirring frequently.
5. Take off the saucepan of milk mixture from burner and through a fine-mesh strainer, strain the mixture into an empty Ninja Swirl pint container.
6. Place the container into an ice bath to cool.
7. After cooling, snap the lid on the pint and freeze for at least 24 hours.
8. After 24 hours, remove the pint from the freezer and take off the lid. Place the Swirl Pint in the outer bowl, then lock the outer bowl lid into place.
9. Transfer the outer bowl into the machine, twisting it into place.
10. Press the power button to turn on the unit. Select Scoop. Then select Gelato.
11. When the program is completed, with a spoon, create a 1½-inch wide hole in the center that reaches the bottom of the Swirl pint container.
12. Add the chopped caramels into the hole and press "MIX-IN" button.
13. Once the program finishes, rotate the outer bowl and detach it from the machine.
14. Transfer the gelato into serving bowls and serve immediately.

Per Serving: Calories: 175 | Fat: 4.2g | Sat Fat: 1g | Carbohydrates: 29.6g | Fiber: 1.1g | Sugar: 26.9g | Protein: 4.7g

Vanilla Chocolate Cookie Gelato

Prep Time: 10 minutes | Cook Time: 6 minutes | Serves: 4

Ingredients:

1 whole vanilla bean, split in half lengthwise and scraped
4 egg yolks
¾ cup heavy cream
⅓ cup whole milk
2 tablespoons brown sugar
1 tablespoon maple syrup
1 teaspoon vanilla extract
5 tablespoons marshmallow paste
5 chocolate cookies, chopped

Preparation:

1. In a medium saucepan, put vanilla bean on burner at around medium-high heat, and toast for around 2-3 minutes, stirring continuously.
2. Turn the heat at around medium-low and whisk in the egg yolks, heavy cream, milk, marshmallow paste, sugar, maple syrup and vanilla extract.
3. Cook for around 2-3 minutes, stirring continuously.
4. Take off the pan of milk mixture from burner and through a fine-mesh strainer, strain the mixture into an empty Ninja Swirl pint container.
5. Place the container into an ice bath to cool.
6. After cooling, snap the lid on the pint and freeze for at least 24 hours.
7. After 24 hours, remove the pint from the freezer and take off the lid. Place the Swirl Pint in the outer bowl, then lock the outer bowl lid into place.
8. Transfer the outer bowl into the machine, twisting it into place.
9. Press the power button to turn on the unit. Select Scoop. Then select Gelato.
10. When the program is completed, with a spoon, create a 1½-inch wide hole in the center that reaches the bottom of the Swirl pint container.
11. Add the cookies into the hole and press "MIX-IN" button.
12. Once the program finishes, rotate the outer bowl and detach it from the machine.
13. Transfer the gelato into serving bowls and serve immediately.

Per Serving: Calories: 347 | Fat: 20.9g | Sat Fat: 4.1g | Carbohydrates: 32.9g | Fiber: 1.5g | Sugar: 21.9g | Protein: 6.6g

Conclusion

The Ninja Swirl by Creami is a game-changer for anyone who loves delicious, homemade frozen treats. Whether you're making milkshake, ice cream, or sorbet, this versatile machine allows you to effortlessly create creamy, satisfying desserts from frozen ingredients. With its easy-to-use design and powerful motor, the Ninja Swirl brings a professional-quality experience into your kitchen.

The accompanying Ninja Swirl Cookbook makes the whole process even easier by offering a variety of mouthwatering recipes tailored to the machine's capabilities. From fruit-based treats to indulgent frozen desserts, the cookbook helps you explore endless flavor combinations while staying within your dietary preferences. It's perfect for anyone, whether you're new to frozen desserts or a seasoned expert in the kitchen.

The Ninja Swirl's quick operation, paired with the cookbook's creative recipes, means you can make nutritious and indulgent treats on the fly. It's an essential tool for busy families, health-conscious individuals, or anyone who enjoys an occasional treat but doesn't want to compromise on quality.

With this user-friendly appliance and the cookbook's guidance, you'll be able to easily craft frozen desserts that are healthier, fresher, and more delicious than anything store-bought. Don't wait to bring the joy of homemade frozen treats into your home—experience the magic of the Ninja Swirl and start creating today!

Appendix 1 Measurement Conversion Chart

WEIGHT EQUIVALENTS

US STANDARD	METRIC (APPROXINATE)
1 ounce	28 g
2 ounces	57 g
5 ounces	142 g
10 ounces	284 g
15 ounces	425 g
16 ounces (1 pound)	455 g
1.5 pounds	680 g
2 pounds	907 g

TEMPERATURES EQUIVALENTS

FAHRENHEIT(F)	CELSIUS (C) (APPROXIMATE)
225 °F	107 °C
250 °F	120 °C
275 °F	135 °C
300 °F	150 °C
325 °F	160 °C
350 °F	180 °C
375 °F	190 °C
400 °F	205 °C
425 °F	220 °C
450 °F	235 °C
475 °F	245 °C
500 °F	260 °C

VOLUME EQUIVALENTS (DRY)

US STANDARD	METRIC (APPROXIMATE)
⅛ teaspoon	0.5 mL
¼ teaspoon	1 mL
½ teaspoon	2 mL
¾ teaspoon	4 mL
1 teaspoon	5 mL
1 tablespoon	15 mL
¼ cup	59 mL
½ cup	118 mL
¾ cup	177 mL
1 cup	235 mL
2 cups	475 mL
3 cups	700 mL
4 cups	1 L

VOLUME EQUIVALENTS (LIQUID)

US STANDARD	US STANDARD (OUNCES)	METRIC (APPROXIMATE)
2 tablespoons	1 fl.oz	30 mL
¼ cup	2 fl.oz	60 mL
½ cup	4 fl.oz	120 mL
1 cup	8 fl.oz	240 mL
1½ cup	12 fl.oz	355 mL
2 cups or 1 pint	16 fl.oz	475 mL
4 cups or 1 quart	32 fl.oz	1 L
1 gallon	128 fl.oz	4 L

Appendix 2 Recipes Index

Made in United States
Orlando, FL
08 July 2025